OPEN UP AND SAY

aaah!

OPEN UP AND SAY

aaah!

Discover...
who you are now

Shape...
who you are becoming

Create...
what you want to experience

ERICA
PEITLER

Circle Takes the Square Publishing
Morristown, New Jersey

Published by Circle Takes the Square Publishing
45 Park Place South #378
Morristown, New Jersey 07960

Publisher's Cataloging-in-Publication Data
Peitler, Erica.

Open up and say aaah!
Discover...who you are now
Shape...who you are becoming
Create...what you want to experience

Erica Peitler. – Morristown, NJ

Circle Takes the Square Pub., 2008.

p. ; cm.
ISBN13: 978-0-9815124-0-2

1. Self-management (Psychology) 2. Self-help techniques. I. Title.

BF632 .P45 2008
158.1-dc22 2008921131

Project coordination by Jenkins Group, Inc • www.BookPublishing.com
Cover and interior design and layout by Eric Tufford

Printed in Singapore
12 11 10 09 08 • 5 4 3 2 1

For Mollie,

Throughout our journey together, your unlimited inspiration and guidance as a life coach and life partner have touched me beyond what words can express. I am honored to put so much of what you have taught me into this piece of work.

Acknowledgments:

The idea for this book was born in Costa Rica, and I would like to acknowledge the Omega Institute's "InSight and InTuition" class I participated in, and especially Brenda Dye, for the gifts of encouragement. Throughout the germination process, I was assisted by an amazing support network and must thank Cathy Roberts, who kept me believing it would come true, eventually. My dear friend Claudia Frankel, you have been a sage and scholar throughout our relationship and have provided me with insights that, to this day, continue to just reach my conscious realization. My friends in the CTI coaching network (Melissa, Kate, Angie, Kim, and Sharon), you have been incredible at holding the space for me to continue to grow into. I am so grateful we have all become friends. To my friends Richard, Glen, Vas, Sandra and Stephanie, all I can say is that you have all showed up in my life with support and encouragement exactly when I needed you most. Thank you! To my lifelong friend Gina, you have been there from the beginning. Thank you so much for your unending confidence and support to "make it happen!"— whatever "it" may be. To Lexa, your confidence in me is instinctual, and I am so appreciative of it. I also must thank my friends at TPH and FK for their welcoming smiles and unending service on this journey.

The Open up and Say aaah! manuscript was written in a small beach cottage in the lovely town of Avon-by-the-Sea, New Jersey. In that special place, I am so thankful to have met and become friends with Francine Reynolds. She has been a wonderful creative mind to bounce ideas around with, and I must credit her with the ultimate selection of the front cover art theme. To Bob Robbins at the Jenkins Group, whom I fell in love with over the phone, thank you for your advice and counsel throughout this process. You quickly saw my dream and vision, and you built a support team for me that has been incredible. To Gwen, I so appreciate your quick mind and ability to cut to the chase and core of the important issues among my stream of delirium. You always kept the big picture in mind. To Eric Tufford, my illustrator whose work is beyond brilliant and who is an absolute delight to collaborate with, thank you so much for your openness and generosity of spirit.

To my parents, thank you for creating the circumstances of my life from which I learned to choose to become the "self" I am today. In my personal view, you have completely fulfilled our "life contract." To Adam, Samantha, and Christine, this journey has brought us so much closer together, and I am so grateful to have you as my family and friends. And last, to Kaitlyn and Caroline, thank you for helping me choose the colors for my logo and for keeping me well stocked with pictures for my refrigerator and desk. You inspire me to remain curious and courageous!

Contents

Foreword

Wouldn't it be great if we knew exactly what is was that we wanted and just went after it? Or what about specifically uncovering what is blocking us or keeping us stuck?

We can go into any bookstore and pick up hundreds of self-help books on the 10 ways to do this, the three keys to that, or the only five things you need to have whatever. They are mainly a directive style of trial-and-error self-help. They offer generalized solutions or popular answers to your problems. And, hey, doesn't everyone want the answers?

The hard truth is we all have different needs and reasons for why things are either working or not working in our lives. We are all individuals, each just as unique psychologically, emotionally, and physiologically as we are genetically.

So how do we get at this uniqueness and get the help we each need and want without years of therapy? Is there a personalized approach we can have access to that would allow us to self-manage the changes in our lives more comfortably and design the happiness we want to experience so we can realize our personal growth potential?

Personalized self-help, just like personalized medicine that specifically targets drug therapy based on recent advances with DNA mapping, could be what makes a breakthrough impact here. What makes personalized self-help different is that it guides you with questions and allows you the space and excitement of finding your own answers. The answers we all need are already inside each of us. We just need access to them!

Open up and Say aaah! is a self-directed, self-coaching book that utilizes a personalized self-help approach. So get ready to explore, discover, and design a practice of aaah! created for you, by you, and in service of you—and your happiness!

How to Use This Book

Life is a completely different experience when it is lived from a mindful, purposeful place of intention setting as opposed to a random existence of hoping for the best. Of course, the latter may appear to be a comfortable place at first, but in reality, you are making a choice to experience limitation. I believe that if you have picked up this book, you are ready to choose and go after more of what you want in your life *now* rather than settling for "what might be some day."

Learning how to manage change within ourselves and around us will have a transformational impact in our lives. It enables us to really go after what we want and therefore allows us to enjoy more of our experiences, whether personal or professional.

Leading our lives on our own terms is the most empowering perspective we can hold. This book, in part, is a *personal leadership journey* from which everyone can benefit. It is about becoming more self-conscious about revealing what really fulfills us and what we want in our lives. Once we know, we will explore how to find the path to get us there. Ultimately, we will arrive at the opportunity for choice and engagement in the experience that we believe will bring happiness for us.

Regardless of our occupations, our obligations, or our socioeconomic statuses, we are all the leaders of our own lives. If you are like most people, you have probably been leading much of your life from a state of unconsciousness. You weren't asleep, but you were just moving along, wishing and hoping that everything would ultimately work out for the best. This can leave you frustrated with and perhaps even resentful of some parts of your life if they are not working out the way you had thought they would.

The questions you need to ask yourself:

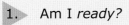

1. Am I *ready?*

2. Am I *able?*

3. Am I *willing?*

"To do what?" you may ask. *To change, grow, and shape your life on purpose*. These questions are in a precise order. To be *ready* requires entering a new state of being. To be *able* requires a clear understanding of skills and systems. To be *willing* requires that you engage in a practice.

Open up and Say *aaah!*

The title *Open up and Say aaah!* refers to opening your heart and mind and finding your voice. It is about building and strengthening your skills of **a**wareness, **a**cceptance, and **a**lignment to guide your choices toward **h**appiness. Aaah! is an acronym for a powerful life tool that will help you face change or challenges with new perspectives. With it, you can mindfully choose your responses and shape your experiences, regardless of the situation or circumstances.

This book has two parts. In Part I, you will be introduced to foundational pieces that will make you "ready and able" to manage yourself through this personalized self-help process. Part II is where you must be "willing" to dig into your current circumstances and the process of shaping your life into what you want to experience—in your way and on your terms!

You may choose to read the book from the beginning and go right through in a linear and progressive way. Or, for those either returning to this process or brave enough to just leap into it, you may want to start with Part Two and the diagnostic section. The choices, you will learn, are always yours!

Part I is designed and written to first introduce you to the concept of **selfhood**, a place you enter by choice, not simply by rite of passage. Here, we begin the process of becoming conscious and purposeful about leading ourselves through the change and growth process in our lives. When we are in a state of selfhood, we are ready to begin to do this. Within the state of selfhood, we will explore several areas that will both prepare us for and provide us with fundamental principles that later will allow us to reach our full potential:

- We will look at the links between health and happiness and highlight the importance of taking ownership for our **self-care**.

- We will discuss techniques for how to be **self-sufficient** and will learn to coach ourselves through the change and growth process.

- We will look at how to build and strengthen our most important relationship in life, the relationship with ourselves, and in doing so will create great **self-reliance**.

- Finally, we will look at how change, growth, and happiness are an integrated system and how we can be **self-empowered** to manage each effectively and comfortably in our lives.

When you understand the elements at work in selfhood, you are ready to step into the leadership role of your life. With the tools provided next, you will be able to begin to work with change and growth to shape your life on purpose and create the happiness you desire.

Part II of this book is an interactive experience and a practical guide through a personalized self-coaching process. Because we all have different learning preferences, you will be offered visual, auditory, and kinesthetic approaches to the activities you will do, to best suit your learning style.

We will begin with a diagnostic tool to identify where you are in the growth and change process for different areas of your life. Once you have completed and scored your personalized assessment, I will frame the findings in the context of an intuitively based change and growth model. You will then engage in exercises to help you identify lost or hidden treasures within yourself. These findings will be extremely useful in your personal journey of seeking, finding, and creating the life you want to experience.

You are the coach here, but I will be on your shoulder and will be whispering in your ear, encouraging you, and supporting you along the way. This is not an easy overnight process. It will, however, be well worth your investment of time if you want to figure out where you are stuck and how to get over it. Like any practice, you will have to try it more than once. I call it **the practice of aaah!**

aaah!

Diagnostic Tool

The diagnostic tool presents a series of
statements requiring a yes or no response.
You may find that taking a position on these
personal issues is challenging or difficult.
If you are true to yourself and answer
honestly, you will create a personalized
assessment that provides insight into a
particular area of your life. Are you in flow
or stuck?

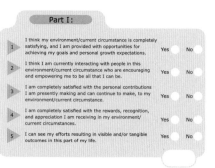

The aaah! Practice Model

The centerpiece of this book is a
unique model that invites you to
explore areas of your life in various
stages of progression. The model has
three phases: the Curious Seeker, the
Courageous Finder, and the Conscious
Creator. Just as life is a holistic set of
experiences, the model recognizes that
we are in all three stages simultaneously.

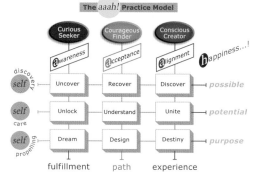

The practice of aaah! brings your awareness capabilities to new levels,
challenges you to accept and be accountable to yourself, and encourages
you to be integrated and aligned with what you want to create and
experience in your life: happiness!

Tools and Treasures

You will coach yourself through the
use of experiential exercises. The tools
are the exercises; the treasures are
the pieces of you that you will find
and reconnect with along the way as
you build up your relationship with
yourself.

In each section, you will be asked to participate in a combination of
exercises that are mind based (encouraging illumination), heart based
(encouraging reflection), or voice based (encouraging expression). Your

diagnostic score will guide you toward the exercises that are right for you. The exercises will not provide you with definitive answers; they will be a *gateway of exploration* from which you will unearth or remind yourself of what you need to know and remember so that you can move forward and shape your life on purpose.

Some of these tools will be familiar, while others will be new. Be open and playful. Try them, even if they initially strike you as silly or you think you already know the answer. There is always something to learn here.

Vital Signs and Signs of Vitality

Throughout the first part of the book, I have included intriguing facts regarding the connections between the dynamics of happiness and health. As the two most universal wants we have as human beings, they are fascinatingly interrelated to each other. These will be referred to throughout the book as Vital Signs and Signs of Vitality.

VITAL SIGNS

Only 6 percent of Canadians and 10 percent of workers everywhere believe that senior management treats people as if they are the most important part of the organization, according to a 2007 Towers Perrin study. The study showed that employees do not believe their organizations or their senior management is doing enough to motivate them to go the extra mile at work and contribute to their companies' success. Firms with the highest percentage of engaged employees increased operating income by 19 percent and earnings per share by 28 percent year over year. Companies with the lowest percentage of engaged employees showed year over year declines of 33 percent in operating income and 11 percent in earnings per share. Only 21 percent of employees worldwide felt engaged.

Source: Towers Perrin, CanWest News Service, 2007

Signs of Vitality

Positive attitude is a key to success. Researchers at the University of Missouri found that happy people, those who frequently experience positive emotions, tend to be more successful and accomplished in many aspects of their lives. Happy people also have success in social relationships; they report having more close friends and being more satisfied with those friendships.

Source: University of Michigan-Columbia. Study published in Psychological Bulletin, December 2005.

There are a few things that this book is not. It is not a book of answers. I do not have the nine things or the seven things you should do to find your happiness. It is also not a book to skim through quickly. This is a book to engage with. You will want to revisit, review, or experience the various exercises several times to fully benefit. You may even come back to it over time to see how things have evolved in your life.

What the book does do is give you aaah-mazing questions to work with and reflect on in an effort to reveal your own answers for creating your happiness. Indulge yourself in those that resonate with you; there is something for you to see, learn, or experience. Skip those that do not seem relevant for now and revisit them later. ***Oh, and remember to bring a notebook along with you on this journey.*** You will be asked to write things and capture some insights. Don't miss this opportunity to "take note" of your personal transformation!

Open up and Say aaah! is both a journey and a life tool. For me, it has been a continuing road map for navigating my personal growth process and shaping my life on purpose.

I hope it will be the same for you.

PART

1

Selfhood

CHAPTER 1 aaah!

Welcome to Selfhood

Life is aaah-mazing! It is full of twists and turns, surprises and disappointments, elations and tragedies—all of which come at us nonstop. Through it all, our challenge is to be open to change and growth so that we can create the lives we want.

We come into this world hardwired with a dream. As children, unencumbered by the complexity of life, this dream imprinted on our hearts may show hints of itself through our early words or actions. It is inside of each of us, and it is waiting for an opportunity for expression.

As life begins to unfold and we get more engaged in the noises and voices of external influences, many of us forget this dream or lose sight of it. The dynamics of the outside world are so much stronger than that little voice inside of us—the original blueprint for our objectives in this lifetime.

Some never get back to that original dream. They are on a path, and life is generally good—so why bother? Others may be haunted and tortured by dreams that were never realized. Perhaps they carry anger and disappointment with them throughout their lives and are convinced that life would have been different, *if only*.

In my own life, I have experienced thoughts and feelings at both extremes. However, I have come to realize that childhood and adulthood represent only the beginning of a progressive passageway to a magical destination called **selfhood**. The secret passwords to get into this magical place are "*I choose*."

In *selfhood*, we get to look at life as it really is and not as we have been told it should be. We learn here that we can create our experiences because they are our responses to the events in our lives. We also learn extensively about the greatest power we have, the *power of choice*. Most important, we realize that life does not operate solely on a go-go and do-do basis. Once we discover the *pause button* in our lives, we can use it to slow down and examine what is going on inside us and around us. So, the magic of selfhood brings with it learning and opportunity. We need to ensure that we are checking in with ourselves to see whether we are, in fact, living a happy life and whether our original dream still has the chance to come forth, at least in its *essence*.

You are about to begin an incredible journey of discovery. For some of you, this may be your first exploration of selfhood. It is magical because it is truly limited only by your own imagination. You are not here by accident, and neither am I.

In order to put the two parts of this book in context, knowing some of my background and how it brought me here might be helpful. Specific stages of childhood, adulthood, and, ultimately, selfhood have provided me with the necessary tools for *self-discovery, self-care,* and *self-propelling* my way forward. You may want to reflect along the way in terms of how your early childhood and adulthood experiences have shaped your entrance into selfhood.

Childhood and the Required *Survival* Skills

Our childhood years provide us with the exposure and learning opportunities to do the personal growth work we came here to do. We may look back on these years with fond memories or disappointment. Either way, those years laid the groundwork for the capabilities we needed to develop to lead fulfilling lives, whether we are choosing to do so or not.

While not tragic, I had a difficult childhood. What I now realize is that everything I have experienced—the good, the bad, the ugly—reveals wisdom, specifically as I have reached *selfhood*.

The most significant childhood lesson I learned early in life was how to emotionally detach from my surroundings. While I was never abused physically, I did suffer emotionally. My parents were young, self-absorbed, freethinking, and verbally expressive. Directness, honesty, and unfiltered expression of thoughts and feelings were the cultural norms in my family. As a child, surviving in this environment of harsh criticism, judgment, and prejudice required me to emotionally disconnect. For protection, I retreated to my head and thoughts for most of my childhood. Rarely would I express vulnerable emotions such as love, compassion, or tenderness. These were not safe expressions in my world, and, in fear of rejection, I shut them down.

I became adept at expressing sarcasm and being confrontational growing up. Later, I came to realize how this was merely a way to further protect myself from allowing others to see my personal hurt and pain.

What has been so important and liberating for me has been the journey back to *reconnecting* with myself. Through this, I have not only benefited from healing childhood wounds but also grown in my emotional connectivity with others. I can now openly engage with and express feelings that I would have avoided when I was younger. This breakthrough has allowed me to be able to share this story with you.

My family life had very few routines or processes. We did not go to church or have a traditional home life with scheduled dinnertimes. We learned to live without structure and to fend for ourselves in most situations. This included most of our meals, homework, and entertainment. We were not a close family, and we moved often. This limited us in forming close friendships. The career aspirations of my father had us moving during my first and last years of high school, times when acceptance and peer community are so important. These were experiences that seemed horrible and deeply sad at the time. Now, with the perspective that time brings, I see that these changes taught me to be independent, adaptable, and flexible. These skills have been invaluable to me throughout my life.

As a young child, I had some health concerns, including a mild heart condition and a leg mobility issue. While surgery theoretically repaired my leg when I was seven years old, a lack of attentiveness to physical therapy left me with limited mobility throughout my life. However, that was also a learning opportunity: I have never let an obstacle, physical or otherwise, get in between me and anything I wanted to do or accomplish in my life. I was an athlete throughout my life and participated in multiple sports teams. I maintain an active life today and continue to push my physical limits to new places. I am not fast, but I can participate in any physical activity I choose. I learned determination and resilience from this experience.

Relationships were not highly regarded by my parents when I was a child, and relationship building was not an investment into which they put time or effort. As a result, I struggled through much of my childhood and adulthood years with some self-limiting beliefs in this area, which kept me from developing strong relationships. A big part of my selfhood development has focused on this important area and rebuilding new sets of beliefs that have enabled my personal growth. Relationships are the fundamental ingredient to creating the experiences we desire, which is what life is all about—not possessions or positions.

I did not experience fulfillment from my home environment, so I sought it elsewhere. Most of my encouragement and recognition during childhood came from my teachers. I was an excellent student and was often given special assignments that acknowledged my leadership and communication skills. Because I was emotionally disconnected from my parents, my teachers represented important role models to me. Gaining their attention and praise was important. While I received plenty of that attention, it was never enough to fill the void I felt inside. Now, of course, I know that this void could be filled only by my own sense of self. We must provide ourselves with the direction, encouragement, and focus we need to achieve our dreams.

Adulthood and the *Drive* Toward Success

My first devastating disappointment as an adult came when I did not get into the college of my choice. The second was not getting the freshman and sophomore grades I needed to go to medical school, which was my childhood dream. I was at a loss about what to do in college: I was a science fanatic and wanted to do something in the health care field. I was thrilled when I stumbled upon pharmacy school. It provided me with a path related to medicine, a professional credential, and the earning power that would allow me to have a comfortable lifestyle. I learned not to leave anything to chance from these experiences. If you want something, be clear, be determined, and don't assume it will just happen—choose to make it happen.

After graduating from pharmacy school, I went into the business side of health care. Having had exposure to the self-medication area during a summer internship, I realized that I had a love and talent for the communication aspects of business. Engaging with consumers and creating educational materials that empowered them in their selection of treatment choices was extremely satisfying. I was a consumer advocate from the beginning and throughout my corporate career. Somehow, I also knew that this had something to do with my purpose in life, but I was not entirely sure what, because it did not look anything like what my dream was as a kid. Try telling a small child that he or she is going to write a self-help book so people can coach themselves through change and growth to find happiness! I have now come to understand that the essence of my dream is "help people be better."

I worked tirelessly throughout my career. I had endless energy, a drive to make money and get promoted, and a constant need to prove that I was worthy of the jobs for which I had been given responsibility. I was also scared to death to slow down and just be with myself. After all, the emotional shutdown I had as a child was still with me, and I instinctively knew that I was not quite ready to deal with that just yet.

In my business career, I distinguished myself as a strong leader and strategic thinker who was not afraid to voice an opinion. This ended up serving me extremely well as I quickly climbed the corporate ladder. I worked at a number of companies throughout my career, and at each one, I always personally connected with the senior managers, found a mentor, and was on the fast track to success.

With success in the business world, I grew even more focused on my career. I saw an endless series of challenges and assignments that I could take on in the areas of transformational change, which had become my specialty. It was a safe place for me because I was good at my work and it kept me constantly busy. I could always find something to fix, change, or create from a blank piece of paper. Leadership also always fascinated me. I would read about it, observe it, practice it, and spend time thinking about how to create and develop my own personalized leadership style. Leadership is not just about a position you hold; to me, leadership is about leading your self-discovery process, leading yourself through the experiences of your life as well as leading others toward their own greatness.

I missed most, of if not all, of my 20s. I was so totally focused on my work. Somewhere in my 30s, I started to wake up, but it was gradual. I found a sweet spot in my career at one company, and with a mentor of mine, I did great work in a partnership that lasted more than 10 years. I was the "go-to girl" and always had exciting challenges to work on. Trying to prove and distinguish myself in my career, I was in a constant state of adrenaline-infused energy. The more I did, there more there was to do. It was an endless stream of strategic projects, turnarounds, and high-profile initiatives, which were always on short time lines with high expectations. For years, I thought I was a cross between a superhero and a strategic wonder kid.

Then, slowly, things started to change. At first, it was hardly noticeable. Over time, though, I really started to think and believe that my gifts and talents were never going to be fully realized in a corporate setting. It was not that I did not have an impact—I did—but it was never enough, and I always wanted more. The intensity I brought to my job was over the top and bordered on an addiction to work. But why was I addicted to my job? Was it the action, the intensity, the power, the challenge—or was it the avoidance of really understanding who I was and what I wanted? Was I on the wrong track for the long term and afraid to face this truth? Better throw myself back into my work double-time and get these scary questions out of my head!

So, I did that, but it ultimately caught up with me. Thankfully, I had begun to prepare for it. I actually knew somewhere in the back of my mind that I was going to have to stop because there could be consequences if I did not. Not immediately, but ultimately I had a deep sense of knowing that my health could be affected by this and that I should be mindful of it. In my own subtle ways, I started to heed this internal advice. In an effort to deal with the pressure, stress, and unfamiliar territory I was entering into psychologically, I started to exercise and diet more. I felt great—better than I had in years. I was getting into shape and making time for me in my life. I learned a valuable lesson about myself: my body was linked to my psyche. When I felt good about my body, I felt good about so much in my life, and when I was not feeling good about my body, I also did not feel good about other things. What an important insight!

Selfhood and the Time to Finally *Thrive*

My transition from adulthood to selfhood started to accelerate during my time as an expatriate in Toronto, Canada. This country had an incredible energy, different from that of the United States, and I was able to really look, see, and experience a different side of life there. The activation of my new levels of awareness really started there in Canada. I was like an iceberg melting, revealing a new part of myself. During this time period, I was faced in rapid succession with three of the toughest choices I would ever make in my life. The first was the initial decision to leave the United States and work in Canada. I was 35 years old, I was in a new and wonderful personal relationship, and life was starting to really take shape. The second decision, about three years later, was not to take a huge promotion that would have required me to live in Europe and that represented a critical stepping-stone in the progression of my career path. What was most unbelievable was that it was on the day that I was scheduled to leave the country and move on to this European assignment that I decided to reverse my decision and say no. It was 7:00 a.m. on September 11, 2001. That day was a day of global and personal transformation.

After having been promoted shortly thereafter to oversee both the pharmaceutical and the consumer health divisions for my company, I was challenged with doing two full-time jobs for more than a year. At that point, I made a choice to strengthen my personal boundaries and work on only one assignment. While not popular with management, it was the right decision for my personal life. After these three major decisions and choices, I knew something was different about me. I now know that I was entering fully, but unconsciously, into the world of *selfhood*. I was getting strong messages of confronting my reality and stepping into more of who I was as a person. I was making tough personal choices and taking positions for myself that revealed my strength of character. I was beginning to uncover the answers to the critical questions of who I wanted to be and what I wanted to experience in this lifetime.

I then returned home to the United States and was promoted again, this time onto the global management team for the company. I was the only female executive and the youngest. After an additional three years of taking on large departmental turnarounds and restructurings, integrating a large acquisition, and developing yet another global company strategy, I started to lose my drive and energy.

During my last 18 months in corporate America, I started to feel that a change was coming in my life. It was so subtle that, at first, I was not sure what it was. It was almost like a general sense of knowing that all this was over in some way, but I could not express it. It was just time. I had a growing sense within me that I needed to move on and explore other things.

I started to journal more regularly and look back on the writing that I had done over the years. Interestingly, there were some patterns. Again and again I wrote that I wanted to be more creative and express myself more. At the same time, I was also beginning to get more in touch with my feelings, and I began to notice more of what was going on around me. I started coaching and working with people in a different way, coming from a deeper place of caring about them. Somehow, I was also starting to care more about and be more at peace with myself. Big pieces inside of me were starting to pry loose. Suddenly, cracks appeared in my protective armor.

In 2005, I took more vacation time than I ever did in my career. This was a clue that, if nothing else, a massive change was on the horizon. I went twice to Canyon Ranch in Tucson, Arizona, for a week, alone. During that special time, I worked out, wrote in my journal, and spent time with myself. I was making some first introductory connections with the real me. The difficult decision, in terms of making the big life move by leaving my job, lay ahead. It was almost incomprehensible in some ways, and yet I had a calling that I could sense. I had been on my personal spiritual journey for some time, but to be at a point where I was intellectually thinking about such a big move and such a big change was incredible. What would I do? What would be next? I had no idea.

Selfhood is an interesting feeling that comes over you. You are instinctively sure about what is right for you to do, but you are not quite able to put it into words. It is like stumbling on a button you can press to put your life into slow-motion or pause while you actually look at what is happening around you. You become an observer, you sense the surroundings, and yet you have some distance and detachment. This feeling, which I first started to really understand at Canyon Ranch, grew stronger and more familiar to me with time. I can call on this state of putting life into "pause" and watch what is happening with keen awareness. Pause is the place where you stop doing and going and allow yourself to just "be" for a moment. Now it seems so natural, and yet it was so unfamiliar to me at this point in my life. I was curious to know and learn more about myself and what was going on in this state of being. Of course, with time, I have come to learn that this was entering into a state of aaah!

Selfhood is also a place of peacefulness, a place where I can explore my desire for creativity and expression and make an emotional reconnection to myself. I am so happy to have arrived here. It has been like landing on planet earth with a fresh set of eyes, along with a desire to try to experience new things. Most important, it has unleashed within me a desire to express myself and, in doing so, to give back to others the gift that was somehow given to me.

I come to this book as someone who has traveled many parts of the world. But the most exciting part of my life so far has been the exploration within myself. It has held the most insight, wonder, and surprise. I am so delighted to share with you these concepts in *Open up and Say aaah!* They have already brought so much to my life, and I believe they will continue to do so. They are practical and simple to use and can have both a subtle and a profound impact. I hope you enjoy your self-discovery process as much as I have enjoyed, and continue to enjoy, mine.

A Healthy and Happy Life

Health and happiness are interrelated, and you have a tremendous amount of control over both. Through your own **self-care**, you not only can shape your change and growth process but you also can choose how to influence your health and happiness experiences.

The questions to ask here are what are you willing to think, feel, and say about it? Yes: think, feel, and say—because your thoughts, your feelings, and your expressed intentions will be your *control panel* for adjusting and influencing your health and happiness.

Taking Ownership and Accountability for *Self-Care*

Self-care is taking ownership and accountability for ensuring that we experience both the health and the happiness we desire in our lives. It is choosing to solicit externally sourced information (learning, advice, and observations) and to elicit internally sourced information (knowledge, wisdom, feelings, and intuition) and integrating it into beliefs and actions that support our overall well-being.

Every day, we have the opportunity to take actions that will have positive effects on our well-being. We know that exercise has enormous benefits for our physical health and it releases endorphins that generate positive emotional benefits. Yet, are we exercising every day? Or even a few days a week? Managing our dietary intake is a no-brainer, right? What about including foods such as blueberries and red peppers into our healthy diets because, in addition to being low in fat and rich with nutrients, they are loaded with antioxidants, which have been linked to preventing disease and improving cognitive function? Would a healthier body and sharper mind make you happy? Our choices for actively engaging in our own self-care are endless. Why wait to correct problems when we have the personal power to prevent them?

Health and happiness are cultural obsessions in this country. We watch news programs about them. We listen to radio reports about them. We worry about them constantly because we are continuously given confusing, conflicting, and evolving information. What have been slower to catch on are the changes we need to be making instead of just listening, watching, and worrying.

After spending most of my adult years engaged in the health care profession and an almost equal amount of time pursuing my own happiness, I finally understand that I am the true owner of both of these dynamics in my life. I am fully accountable for my self-care. What I take into my body, how I engage in my own self-talk, the safety precautions I choose to take, the rest I allow myself to get, the relationships I form, the way I exercise, the emotional eruptions I allow myself to indulge in—these are all decisions within my absolute control in the management of my own self-care. *I am the only one who can and will create what I want to experience in my life, including my health and happiness.* You have to take care—***self-care***—of yourself.

VITAL SIGNS

Employees' engagement has a dramatic impact on their health and psychological well-being, according to a recent Gallup study. Among engaged employees, 62 percent feel that their work lives positively affect their physical health, compared with 39 percent of nonengaged employees. In addition, 54 percent of actively disengaged employees say they think their work lives are having a negative effect on their physical health. Regarding psychological well-being, 51 percent of actively disengaged employees feel their work lives are having negative effects on them, compared with only 20 percent of nonengaged workers and just 6 percent of engaged workers.

Source: Gallup Management Journal, "Employee Engagement Index," January 2005

Signs of Vitality

Happy employees show up to work. A recent survey by business information firm CCH Inc. found that organizations where employees ranked morale as "fair" or "poor" had a higher level of absenteeism than those companies whose employee morale was ranked "good" or "very good."

Source: CCH, Inc., "2007 CCH Unscheduled Absence Survey"

Being accountable for our personal health and happiness is a far bigger responsibility than many of us care to take on. To be effective, we need to actively demonstrate interest, discipline, practice, and continuous conscious decision making. We must really believe in what we are doing and why we are doing it. It is certainly easier to deflect, ignore, and make a series of excuses about why these elements of self-care are not possible. We also find it natural to take more of an interest in, or even misplaced ownership for, the health and happiness of others before or instead of our own. Then, there are those who prefer to swallow their own frustrations and keep themselves in a state of projected outer control, falsely believing that this constitutes managing their health and happiness. It does not. That is simply an attempt to either ignore these things in their lives or hide the truth from others as well as themselves. *There is no place for any of us to hide.* If we resist the expression of our emotions or deny ourselves the attention we need, the end result will be negative health consequences. We need to understand our roles and believe in the importance of our own self-care.

Health and Happiness: The Eye of the Beholder

"Health" and "happiness" are not words to throw around and take for granted. They are fundamental and universal wants and needs. Yet, they are unfortunately not well understood. Part of the reason lies in the fact that they are personal and subjective experiences. So, what is healthy and happy to one person could look like sick and depressed to another. This may be hard to understand or believe, but we see examples of it every day.

How can people we know and love be so positive and energetic, seemingly enjoying every moment in life, when they are battling cancer? How can completely healthy young people, with their whole lives ahead of them, be so frustrated and unhappy that they need to take drugs to function in the world?

As human beings, we have the choice to define our targeted experiences and then literally create them. Yet, with so much choice and control, look at what many of us do. We choose to sleepwalk through our lives, dismiss our creative control, and dodge accountability for the outcomes we experience. We are not intentionally irresponsible—but rather we are not clear or even aware of how much influence we actually have to manage the challenges and changes in our lives and to create the experiences we want. We have been given scripts and a set of beliefs that have trapped us into our current expectations that this is just the way life goes. So we either resist or, worse, completely surrender to the disruptions of change and the unexpected twists and turns. We just take for granted that what happens is meant to be, and we have our happy and our unhappy days, weeks, or years. While this may seem a little extreme, the question is whether we want to *participate in the process of creating the happy and healthy experiences for ourselves or relinquish choice for chance.* Changing our beliefs about what is possible takes focus and commitment; it also requires some learning about how to approach it. Later, we are going to spend some time specifically working with changing our beliefs so that they empower us to go after and have the experiences we want. Our degree of involvement in our self-care will determine this for our health and happiness.

Health and Happiness ... the Power of *AND*

Health and happiness, when we consciously think about them, can never really be either/or considerations — we want both (at the same time, which we later come to realize). In our early years, we focus on happiness and believe that our health is a natural or a given. So we strive, work, and look to achieve the goals that we believe will lead us to what we want, whether or not we refer to this overtly as our happiness. Much later on in the process, some of us realize that happiness is a choice that we can have at any moment and is not an endpoint possession or a destination at which we ultimately arrive. Unfortunately, this awareness comes at about the same time many of us are reminded of the fragility of health, either through our own health challenges or those of the people close to us. It may shake us up enough so that our focus shifts exclusively to the health side of the spectrum. Realizing what is really at risk, we declare our desire and intention for our health and shift our priorities to reflect that. We believe that being healthy will make us happy—and for a while, perhaps it will. However, what we can also do, through our self-care choices, is decide that we want both our health and our happiness as independent and interdependent experiences. We can negotiate the "and" upfront by stating our intentions for both, and we can ensure that we mindfully make the changes we need to create the experiences of both.

Hard and Soft Health Care

To me, describing the relationship between health and happiness is like describing the differences between the technical function of our heart's ability to pump blood throughout the body and the "psychological" experience of being able to emotionally feel and express the love in our heart. One is a mechanical, measurable, and involuntary activity; the other is subjective, impossible to measure, and completely voluntary. The functional parts are what I call *hard* health, and the subjective, emotional experiences are referred to as *soft* health.

Hard health care is what we can see and measure, such as cholesterol levels, blood pressure, and fasting glucose or sugar levels. It could also be benign polyps found during a routine colonoscopy or a mass found on an X-ray. You might even consider it to be the body mass index (BMI), which defines whether you are the right weight, or the skin cancer screening your dermatologist may do.

Our health care system is great at finding, diagnosing, and prescribing treatments for many hard health care issues. We are advancing in defining pre-disease stages and risk factors for the future development of diseases and even providing interventions, such as balloon angioplasty for a clogged artery before a heart attack occurs. We are even more aggressive now in putting high-risk patients on medications and nutritional supplements earlier to prevent diseases from occurring in the first place.

Signs of Vitality

Positive attitude is a key to success. Researchers at the University of Missouri found that happy people, those who frequently experience positive emotions, tend to be more successful and accomplished in many aspects of their lives. Happy people also have success in social relationships; they report having more close friends and being more satisfied with those friendships.

Source: University of Missouri-Columbia. Study published in Psychological Bulletin, December 2005.

VITAL SIGNS

Signs of Vitality

But what about the connection between how we feel about ourselves, our lives, and our relationships and how those feelings affect our health profile? What we often fail to consider is the damage or stress we cause in our bodies when we are unhappy. What happens when we are angry, frustrated, lonely, anxious, bored, or generally discontented with our lives on an ongoing basis? What happens when the job is not right, the relationships are not supportive, the pressure is just too much to handle, and we feel we are trapped? There are real physical and emotional detrimental effects.

The science of human physiology is dedicated to studying the functions and processes that occur in the body. More than ever, relationships are being found between the cause and effect of hormones and emotional feelings, which have real consequences, both positively and negatively, on the body. In fact, for many illnesses, such as depression, drug therapy is designed to counterbalance these hormonal responses. While many people may be walking around with normal cholesterol and blood pressure levels, if they are depressed, research shows that they also have a higher likelihood of having a heart attack.

Soft health care is the connection between what we think, how we feel, and whether we characterize ourselves subjectively as being happy, fulfilled, and emotionally in balance. The effects of these issues on our overall health care profile are just as real in terms of impact and meaning, even though they are not often outwardly visible or easy to measure.

Our thoughts and feelings have profound effects on our health status. We know that the power of positive thinking can cure or reverse negative health effects, and we are inspired when we hear stories of how people have overcome illness or hardship. But what about the potential for the power of negative thinking to likewise cause damage to our health?

Consciously or unconsciously, if you are unhappy, you are causing a negative stress experience on your body. It may show up in different ways, in different degrees, and at different times, but it will show up. So, simply stated, here is **your wake-up call:** if you do not acknowledge your unhappiness and address it like you would a physical health issue, you may be shortening your life!

The point is: if you are happy, great! Don't worry about measuring and managing it; just enjoy it. But if you are stuck and can't seem to get there in the first place, that's a different concern. In this case, wouldn't it be great to have some help in finding out where you are stuck and how to get moving forward again? This is the question we need to be asking ourselves. The practice of aaah! provides you with a life tool that gives you a way to identify and measure your progress in the change process in a visual and compelling way. You will learn questions and skills that will assist you in coaching yourself into a purposefully chosen state of happiness— a state of aaah!

aaah! The Impact of Self-Talk on Self-Care

Have you ever thought to yourself that you were stupid, couldn't do anything right, or didn't deserve something? Have you ever beat yourself up, over and over again, inside your head, for prolonged periods of time? Did you think that was just a private little conversation you were having with yourself with no consequences? Think again.

Our self-talk has a powerful effect on our bodies. Sometimes we can be extremely encouraging and positive by acknowleding ourselves when we have accomplished something important. This is an empowering tool that can increase our energy, optimism, or general well-being, and we will spend more time on this later. Most of the time, however, this self-talk has a negative tone—a victim consciousness or the voice of the saboteur. Through this voice and with abusive and toxic language, we create for ourselves a hostile living environment, and we inflict negative thoughts that affect our bodies, even though the conversations are going on only in our heads!

For those of you who exercise, eat right, and get a good amount of rest but who also talk to yourself negatively, be mindful that your body is a whole system. You can't expect to be healthy if you just do a few good things to the outside but don't take care of the inside. This is why the mind and body connection is so important. To have a healthy and happy life, we need to take a holistic view of our self-care.

What you see in your outside world is a reflection of what you are creating in your inside world. Change your mind and your thoughts and you change your feelings and beliefs. Ultimately, you change your view of your world, and your world therefore changes. This is what is meant by our ability to create our experiences.

The Health Care Model
Can Teach Us about *Happiness*

On the basis of my many years of experience as a health care insider, when I listen to macro issues related to health care being discussed from an emerging science and policy perspective, I repeatedly hear several major themes. What I find interesting is how these health care themes relate closely to happiness themes as well. Here are some observations:

> **1.** *We debate and believe we want access to universal health care—what about access to universal happiness?*

We have the opportunity every day and every moment to choose to be happy in our lives. Happiness is a state of being, an experience we create for ourselves. It is our appreciation for life, our joy of observing the wonders and beauty around us, our excitement to do the jobs we love, and the fun we have playing Frisbee with our puppies. Happiness possibilities are all around us. So, what gets in our way? We already have universal access to happiness, and there are no predetermined criteria for inclusion. It is our personal choice, if and when we are ready to choose it and experience it.

> **2.** *Personalized medicine is an emerging frontier—what about personalized self-help?*

Mapping the human genome has provided the scientific and medical communities with insights on how to better target medical solutions to individual treatment needs and conditions. This is an exciting breakthrough! We now have the ability to avoid wasted time and costs as well as negative side effects in the old trial-and-error format of medicine, and we can now be more certain about what is more likely to work in someone's personalized condition on the basis of his or her unique DNA and genetic makeup.

How about a personalized approach to managing change in our lives and designing the happiness we want to experience? Wouldn't it be great if we could understand exactly what it was that we wanted and go after it? Or what about specifically uncovering what is blocking us or keeping us stuck? We can go to any bookstore and pick up hundreds of self-help books on the 10 ways to do this, the three keys to that, the five things you need to have this. They are mainly a directive style of trial-and-error self-help. They offer generalized solutions or popular answers to your problems—and, hey, doesn't everyone want the answers?

We all have different needs and reasons for why things are either working or not working in our lives. We are all individuals, each just as unique psychologically, emotionally, and physiologically as we are genetically.

So how do we get at this uniqueness and get the help we need? The key difference with personalized self-help is that it guides you with questions and allows you the space and excitement of finding your own answers. The answers we all need are already inside each of us.

3. *While the health care model searches for blockbusters, we are looking for box-busters for happiness!*

The blockbuster drug for a pharmaceutical company is the home run. This breakthrough, patented medicine allows a drug company to offer a new solution, usually for a high-profile disease, to millions of people and charge a premium for it so it can fund and support additional research projects. It is the foundation for how this industry has operated in the past. The challenge is that these blockbusters are now few and far between and the new process of using DNA mapping to develop more personalized medicine is now changing the game to be more specific and targeted.

In the world of seeking our happiness, we are looking for breakthrough solutions as well. What we need is a question or an insight to get us out of the self-limiting or **boxed-in belief** that is separating us from what we want. We need a **box-buster**! The currently ingrained belief system that has us trapped in seeing the world through a specific lens either does not work or no longer applies to us.

We are looking for these box-busters to give us different perspectives or reflective awakenings and a new way to look at our lives, and bring our desired experiences into sharp focus. Once we are released from being trapped by our old self-limiting boxes, we are able to try new things and discover alternative possibilities to get to where we want to go.

VITAL SIGNS

According to the American Lung Association, colds account for more visits to the doctor than any other condition. Adults suffer an average of two to four colds per year.
Source: American Lung Association, 2008

Signs of Vitality

People who are happy, lively, or calm or who exhibit other positive emotions are less likely to catch a cold when exposed to the virus, and they are also less likely to report symptoms when they do get sick.
Source: Carnegie Mellon University, 2006

From Life-Saving Tools to *Life-Shaping* Tools

Medicine has made what used to be life-threatening situations survivable. Where would we be today without antibiotics, mobile defibrillators, CPR techniques, or even aspirin? These powerful life-saving tools are now widely available to help us to overcome daily threats.

While seemingly less urgent, although no less important, what about tools we can use to avoid stress and gain access to happiness? At times, I know that I might be in a situation where I can feel anger or adrenaline starting to build up nervously in my body and I am ready to activate the fight-or-flight system. What do we do in these situations, and what tools do we have to avert an emotional eruption? Well, breathing deeply and counting to 10 are possible interventions to attempt to calm us down in the moment, but those techniques, in many cases, are not going to be enough. The aaah! practice model offers tangible tools that can be available to you in these situations. You will learn that the **acronym aaah!** is, in fact, a toolbox for helping you to shape your life on purpose in those moments. Specifically, you will learn about the powerful skills of **awareness, acceptance,** and **alignment,** which will provide you with access to and perspective for looking immediately at these same situations in a different light. So, a more grounded and clearer understanding of how to choose what you want to experience can be created by you in that moment. Situations that would have previously resulted in emotional disruption can be handled with curiosity, calmness, and learning when the aaah! practice tools are used. This can have positive consequences associated with it, because the adrenaline burst, the negative emotional response, and the postexplosive toxic cleanup can all be avoided. You are going to find that opening up and saying aaah! every day is good for both your health and your happiness!

VITAL SIGNS

Depression has reached massive proportions. In any given year, nearly 10 percent of the population, or about 20.9 million American adults, suffers from a mood disorder. Depression is the number-one cause of disability in those aged 18 to 44, according to a report from the National Institute of Mental Health.

Source: National Institute of Mental Health, Archives of General Psychiatry, 2005, World Health Report, 2004.

Signs of Vitality

Abusive bosses cause depression. Researchers at Florida State University found that employees who were in an abusive work relationship experienced more exhaustion, job tension, nervousness, depressed moods, and mistrust. In addition, they were also less likely to work longer or on weekends. Employees were more likely to leave because of an abusive boss than because of pay issues.

Source: Florida State University, December 2006

To: **Business Leaders**

Subject: **The Business Case for Health and Happiness**

Without exception, health care is a priority agenda item for both individuals and institutions, yet the focus on happiness is currently the concern of individuals only. The tremendous opportunity for change here can have far-reaching benefits, given that health and happiness are seemingly connected. The amazing part of this is that the solution for both the health care crisis and our individual obsessions for pursuing our happiness is the same.

In looking at the health care side only for a moment, most individuals are concerned about affording health care insurance, and companies, facing escalating insurance costs, are shifting more of the burden of paying for health care benefits onto their employees. In some cases, companies are also either offering incentives to those employees practicing healthier behaviors, such as exercising, weight management, and getting regular checkups, or charging premiums to employees practicing high-risk behaviors, such as smoking or being overweight. Even now, in some companies, we see the emergence of wellness coaches, who encourage people to better manage their health care risks. So the need to manage costs has forged an apparent "collaboration" between individuals and organizations as it relates to the observable and measurable parts of the health care equation. But this is only part of the challenge. Asking people to take greater care of themselves through the actions of making lifestyle and behavioral changes, even while helping them measure it, will bring only short-term to mid-term results. A major piece is missing.

When we look at the happiness side of the equation, individuals are on their own, with organizations claiming that this is not their business. But is that a good business perspective to have? If being happy leads to greater health and wellness, as well as more productive and committed employees, the business case for individual and organizational collaboration may already be more than obvious.

If that is not compelling enough, let's examine, as an example, the two biggest challenges being faced in corporate America today beyond the rising cost of health care.

First is the talent management challenge.

Getting well-qualified people to join and stay with your organization is critical if you are a business leader. Today, however, the demands of business on the lives of individuals are more significant than ever. Many people are choosing not to do anything and everything to climb the corporate ladder; they have more of a desire for work-life balance and personal downtime. People are increasingly concerned about their stress management and the long-term health effects of pushing themselves beyond reasonable limits. Stress, as we will discuss later, is a reaction to resistance—resistance to change.

I would submit that companies taking more of an active interest in the offering of not only health benefits but also happiness benefits would serve to enhance the commitment of talented employees to their respective organizations. ATMs, laundry services, and meal options are amenities that attempt to ease the burden of life for employees, but these are not exactly the same as helping them find fulfillment and happiness in their lives, which includes the enormous amount of time invested in their professional work. More than ever before, winning the "war on talent" in the future will have more to do with winning their hearts through their overall happiness and well-being.

Second, the speed of business and transformational change only continues to accelerate.

Most people resist change, so they are often not willing or not well equipped to embrace fast-moving organizational changes, which can slow down the competitiveness of a business.

Successful organizations of the future will need to invest in a new style of change management initiatives. They will be interested in collaborations with their workforces that invest in getting them better ready, able, and willing to manage the changes in their own lives through a focus on happiness. They will do this with a conscious understanding that this will have a tremendous ripple and spillover effect into the health and wellness of their business, both from reducing health care costs and from increasing productivity. Building organizational capabilities in individual change management will better prepare employees for faster adoption of changes in the business world. The goodwill offered through this will further serve to motivate employees as well as increase their commitments to their organizations.

aaah!

Now back to the critical linkage between health and happiness. Most people want to avoid change, whether it is coming toward them from an organization's perspective or in service of their own personal happiness, although the latter is, of course, likely to be preferred. And yet, the dynamics of change are the same for both.

The benefits of investing in employee happiness would result in creating a workforce that understands and accepts change management principles on a personal level, assists in managing the stress of change, which could have negative health consequences, and increases commitment of employees to organizations. It's win-win-win—a happy solution with health benefits and performance-related outcomes.

So, there is little doubt that building capability for change management with a focus on individual happiness will have a direct effect on shaping the future for both the individual and the organization. However, many will probably be slow to adopt this.

At the intersection of health and happiness lies the solution both parties need to embrace yet on which both fail to focus. The current focus is behavior modification, and the new focus for real change needs to be belief modification along with behavior modification. Behavior modification is where we focus because we can objectively define it and in many ways attempt to measure it. The concept of belief modification is more elusive to understand and measure, but it is the far more critical and valuable change to make when considering long-term sustainability.

Perhaps this is where the change management philosophy needs to change. Having the trust and faith that efforts that help people understand what and how their beliefs contribute to their experiences is well worth the investment. "Why?" you may ask. Well, first of all, consider the alternative. Behavior modification is great until a challenge comes along. If a foundational belief does not support that behavior, it is vulnerable. The chance to binge on your diet or smoke that cigarette boils down to willpower. When a belief is supporting you, you have an undeniably strong hold on your behavior; you just do not believe that it is appropriate or right for you to behave in another way. You are not vulnerable at all, so you are stubbornly going to find ways to defend your beliefs.

An example of this is not being willing to drive once you have had a drink. Some people either will just not drink or, if they have had a drink, will get another person to drive them home, period. We need to apply the use of the concept of belief modification to more situations than we currently do. An empowering belief of possibility will break through all limitations.

While you may not be able to measure whether the belief is in place initially, you will have a longer-term sustainability of the behavior modification if it is supported by the belief change. So whether in service of health or happiness, belief modification is the common missing link that will need to be brought forward . We will soon learn about the dynamics of changing our beliefs as well as coaching ourselves through the process.

So the business case for happiness does seem apparent, and if health and happiness derive their connectedness from the same source of change, why not provide individuals with the meaningful missing link? With both individuals and organizations looking to do all they can to manage escalating heath care costs, managing happiness and well-being appears to be an important place to look.

Managing ourselves through the continuous changes in our lives requires us to take care of ourselves. Self-care is our link to creating happy and healthy lives. It encompasses our physical, emotional, intellectual, and spiritual energy as well as our sense of overall well-being. As we continue through this journey, we need to be mindful that happiness is not only the positive joy we seek in pursuit of our dreams and aspirations but also a controllable lever in managing our health and wellness.

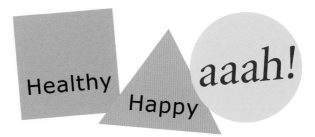

CHAPTER 3 *aaah!*

Coach Yourself!

The acknowledgement of *self-care* as the integrating force between health and happiness puts our lives just where we want them: *in our own hands*. But how can we skillfully manage our dynamic environments and the volatility of our emotions while pursuing personal desires and maintaining focus and control? What tools are available that allow us to be **self-sufficient** in managing our personal change and growth process?

Learning to coach yourself is a great start! By understanding foundational concepts about the mind-set of coaching, you'll be better equipped to apply the process to yourself. Throughout this chapter, I will provide you with a dozen coaching tips and will give you tools and techniques to help you work through the self-coaching process. This will build your skills and confidence in becoming your own coach and advocate as you navigate through your real-life conditions using the practice of aaah!

Whether you have recently been thrust into a challenging transition or setback, are confused about what you want right now, or are just bored and ready for something new, you will be able to coach yourself through any stage of your life.

At times during this process, you may want to consider your need for outside support. As a professional leadership coach, I certainly believe in the benefits of an interactive coaching relationship, even though the approach here is designed for those who want to self-direct their process, at least initially. Perhaps you are not yet ready for outside

All of your coaching efforts should be centered on a goal you have set. Decide what your goal is and what it will feel like to experience it. Then commit to realizing it. **Remind yourself of your goal frequently.** While life is dynamic and our coaching will need to be flexible in terms of working with whatever shows up in our lives, we want to have consistent focus on our goal, or happiness target. As you move through your day, ask yourself, "What is here for me now?" As coach, you need to look for the learning and insights that surround your daily activities to support the realization of your goal.

collaboration with a coach or maybe you do want to supplement the work you are doing here with outside assistance. All of these options are reasonable. Even so, you will not be totally alone in this process. In addition to your own guidance and mine, you will soon be joined by others you choose to include for support in your practice of aaah!

My goal is to get you comfortable with being your own coach. You may know that coaching is also a leadership style. Consciously or unconsciously, you may already have significant coaching experience through your initiatives in business, raising children, or working with associations or other organizations. If you do, we will sharpen some of your skills. If this is new to you, relax. Coaching skills are great life skills from which we can all benefit.

To Start, Just Say When

It is no surprise that the human condition is to resist change, even if it keeps us from our own happiness. Being able to express awareness about being stuck in our lives is not uncommon. While some of us struggle and work ourselves into emotional turmoil and distress over this, others are quite content just to stay there. They are not happy, but they are also not motivated to change because what they have is *good enough* for them.

Are you looking for more than just good enough in your life? Will you *be willing* to develop a practice to get you through the change and growth process so you can experience the happiness you want? Those who will benefit most from this approach in coaching themselves are prepared to challenge their own beliefs and behaviors, they are able to ask the tough questions, and they are willing to act on the answers to pursue a life that is fulfilling.

What you have done before or where you have been in your life prior to this moment does not matter. If you are ready to *seek, find, and create* your life from this point forward, *this is the place to be*.

You can shape and change your life whenever you are ready to start, and being ready to start is a personal decision. There is no judgment here. When you want to make the choice of moving forward with your life in a new way, you will. Until then, you can wait for a lightning bolt of inspiration, or you can choose to move forward on faith.

Inside-Out Readiness

Life is complicated, in part, because we make it that way. Getting caught up in a whirlwind of conflicting agendas is easy to do. There is the outside world and our internal world of expectations. Unfortunately, the outside world dominates because it is loud, always present, and brutally clear about its judgments and labels. That small internal voice of ours is often dwarfed by the bravado and strength of those who have an opinion, claim to know the answers, and just want to solve our problems— *their way.*

In coaching, the first thing to acknowledge is that all of our answers are already within us. We don't need other people to solve our problems or impose their solutions. We need to listen to our internal voices, and we need to be able to reflect on insightful questions to help reveal these answers to ourselves more clearly. *You must be willing to be coached, by yourself.*

Listening is a coaching tool that operates on several levels. Here, we are using a self-directed approach, so we need to get connected to ourselves and really **turn up the volume on our inner wisdom and intuition.** We need to find a quiet place to be and become centered, and we need to allow for the time and space to go inside ourselves. This will take practice to get comfortable with, but it holds profound insight for us. We also need to be alert to and listening for the messages we receive from interactions with others and from observations in the environment. Outside listening is a 360-degree process; messages can come from anywhere and can completely surround us. So listen in, up, and around.

Coaching Tip 2

Listen inside and Out

This may be either surprising or comforting, but the truth is that all the answers we need are already within us. What we need is access to the answers. We gain this through a combination of **asking ourselves the right questions,** giving ourselves time to process them, managing our ego/gremlin negative voices, and empowering our wisdom or positive inner voice to be heard.

In coaching, questions are our most powerful tools. While our answers are within, access to them will need to be inspired by well-placed questions that cause us to reflect or illuminate what is here, now, or next. Our best questions are those that focus on the what and how while leaving the whys out. The what and how questions are in the now and next time frames. Looking at the whys takes us back, not forward, and challenges us to rationalize ourselves, which could also activate our negative self-talk. **Stay focused on the what and how questions,** and don't be afraid to give yourself huge, crazy, and inspiring questions to chew on over a period of time. These inquiries can often lead to powerful breakthroughs. Example:

Weaker question:
• Do you feel overwhelmed right now?

Stronger question:
• How does feeling overwhelmed offer you an entry point for trying something new and different now?

To coach yourself effectively, you need to be fully present with yourself. This means being grounded and having your mind, heart, and voice all in the same place. It also means listening to yourself and being focused on your goal. In addition, sometimes you might be present but not stepping into your "bigness." That means that you are allowing yourself to play small with safe choices. When you sense this in yourself, you need to call yourself forth into the aaah-mazing you, **where your possibilities are unlimited and your potential is enormous for living large in your life.** You are a beautiful and magnificent being! Coach yourself to fill up the expansive space with your life experiences.

Getting the Right Mind-Set in Place

At its most basic level, coaching is about asking questions, listening, and being present. In part, it will be like being a great friend to yourself. Of course, coaching is more than this: it is also about seeing greatness and calling it forth, in others or in ourselves. We all have the capability for aaah-mazing things; we just forget to **"play big"** sometimes and allow ourselves to settle for less than we are capable of becoming. I call that "playing small." As coaches, we cannot let ourselves get away with playing small. We are here to live our lives in the biggest way possible, you wouldn't want to stop short of anything less than your dreams and desires.

Similarly, we should be honest and truthful with what is. We need to be able to challenge ourselves and recognize when we have our ego, gremlin, or saboteur at work distracting us from our best interests and directing us toward self-limitation and fear. Doing this effectively takes diligence, honesty, and commitment to mindfulness. Coaching yourself is not going to be easy. It requires calling yourself into an active state and summoning your mind, heart, and voice to work with you as you process your experiences and learning. Unfortunately, there are no shortcuts—just hard work. Because we are coaching ourselves, who would we fool, anyway? No sense rationalizing, deluding, and creating meaningless distractions for ourselves, unless we just want to stay stuck!

Coaching Creation versus Competition

Many of you have spent a good part of your life checking out the Joneses. You know them: they're the friends, neighbors, or colleagues who, in your opinion, always seem to have unbelievably great things happen to them. If only your life were so good, being happy would be easy.

We all have challenges. Remember that most of our lives are not visible to the outside world, and likewise, we cannot see what others are experiencing. So, while things may appear easier for some, comparing ourselves to others serves no purpose. In jealousy, we stir up the unproductive energy of competition versus creation. Competition has its place, but in terms of experiencing a fulfilling life, we need to shift our focus to **creation**. There is enough for everyone in the world—**true abundance**. You need to coach yourself to stay focused on what you want to create in your life. Don't worry about those Joneses!

If you catch yourself comparing your life or situation to that of others in a negative way, stop and acknowledge it. Then, consciously remind yourself that you are focused on creating and experiencing your life, not anyone else's.

Are you getting nervous, thinking you are not a creative person? No need to worry—the type of creation we are referring to here requires only your thoughts and desires. Of course, that may not be the only reason you are nervous. You may also be thinking, "I am not happy right now, but there are really good reasons why." And you can prove it, right? I bet you can, too—because you have a well-developed *story*, don't you? Your story is that automatic and well-rehearsed speech or monologue that explains, justifies, and reconfirms exactly why your life is the way it is. You know: *your story*!

Coaching Tip 6
Meet Yourself Where You Are

Before you jump in to coach yourself on an issue, notice first where you are, and get in touch with how you are feeling. Notice your energy, thoughts, and emotions. After checking in with yourself, choose to coach yourself from where you are right now. So, for example, if you are frustrated, allow yourself to see what the frustration has for you in terms of learning in this moment. Don't just rush to say, "Hey, I will just ignore this and get positive now!" and put the frustration behind you. We may instinctively want to jump into a direction or a solution. Try to avoid this temptation and allow yourself to get grounded in the coaching. Then you can meaningfully move forward, choosing where you may need to go next from a centered position—that is, if you need to go anywhere. **Be open to staying where you are, too!** Just being with an experience for a while can often be the best option for creating clarity and closure so we can move forward.

34

Coaching Tip 7

Actively Manage Your Self-Talk

As we listen to ourselves, we need to be able to distinguish between our positive inner wisdom self-talk and our ego-based, saboteur, or gremlin negative self-talk. The negative self-talk will focus our attention on fear and self-limiting beliefs. It will keep us stuck if we don't self-coach and immediately stop it when it shows up. We should ask ourselves, "Who is this? Can I name this voice? Is it trying to look after me and keep me safe, or is it reinforcing old belief systems out of fear?" Ask your internal intuitive voice to guide you. **Listen to your heart and quiet your mind chatter.** You need to take an active role in quieting the negative voices, or even the positive, coercive ones that try to hold you back, and amplifying the positive voices within that expand your possibilities and move you forward.

My story was a compelling piece of drama about how people just didn't understand me. If they did, they would see why I pushed so hard, what a great leader I was trying to be, and how I was *right* about so many things.

That story served me in only one way: to create delusions and illusions around what was really going on with me. I was stuck, and I did not really understand myself. Trust me: you have a powerful story and probably a set of stories for the different areas of your life. This may be hard for you to unwind and unravel, but we will get there. Be prepared to step in as the coach and challenge yourself on your own story. Later we will spend time rewriting your story and changing it into something that empowers, as opposed to limits, your life. You need to be a strong coach because to ignore or brush off something as trivial or to outsmart yourself is to choose to stay stuck.

So let's really commit to rewriting that story together, okay?

Coaching Circulinear Learning

We have all overcome obstacles multiple times only to return, yet again, to that same place where we apparently started. This is why our story is so practiced—we've been through it before. But when we are unconsciously wandering through our lives and making random choices, we are riding the mindless merry-go-round. Acquiring a keen sense of awareness, which is the first step, or entry point, into the process of change and growth, allows us to evolve to where we can experience our learning more consciously. I call this concept **circulinear learning**.

The concept of circulinearity takes into account that we come at the same things in our lives several times as we are experiencing changes, learning, and growth. The importance of understanding this, however, is that we are never really in the same place twice. We are always moving up and forward, even when similar situations may seem familiar and repetitive. With awareness of circulinear learning, you begin to see that you are constantly **breaking things down** so you can look at them more closely, and you are **breaking through** old self-limiting belief systems into new possibilities, embodying the changes and learning as ingredients in your personal growth. We need to understand this concept as we coach ourselves. With awareness, each time we experience a similar situation, we need to explore with curiosity the question of "*What is **here now** for us?*" What is subtly or significantly different in this space and time? Taking the time to observe and reflect will fuel our circulinear learning trajectory.

You Are the Coach

Coaching is sometimes a messy process. It is not linear, and this self-coaching approach, in particular, requires you to be fully engaged, because you have all the answers. I know this seems hard to believe right now. If you had the answers, you would be solving your problems already, right? Well, maybe. The concept of solving problems is a loaded one.

At
times,
we might
slip into old
unconscious behaviors
or surrender to our negative
self-talk. In these moments, **we
will need to challenge ourselves or
name a truth we may be avoiding.** This
is constructive tough love, not an invitation for
our gremlins, egos, or saboteurs to come out and have
a group party. We need to be mindful of our approaches and
ensure that we are encouraging our personal growth
rather than beating ourselves up. Consider the
reality of where you are right now, ask
yourself what you need to say or do to
break through to you, and give
yourself what you need, out
of love and in service
of the goal
you have
set.

Coaching Tip 8
Be Alert to Your Need for Tough Love

Coaching Tip 9
Experience the Full Range of Your Emotions

Life
is a
full range
of experiences,
with both highs and
lows. We need to embrace
the entire continuum. If we
do not allow ourselves to feel the
extremes, we are denying ourselves the
opportunity to experience a full life. We need to
coach ourselves to allow these experiences to unfold,
even if they appear to be uncomfortable at first. **The pain
we feel on the downside will be balanced by the
ability to reach new high levels on the upside.**
Take the opportunity to expand the breadth and
depth of your feelings and experiences.
This also includes allowing ourselves
to express positive and
negative emotions in an
appropriate way
across the full
range.

In my approach to coaching, you are not broken, and we don't need to fix anything. We do, however, need to reveal and discover things. This may not be a straightforward exercise. Trust the process here. Don't get too attached to any expectations. Stay focused on what you want, and let go of concerns for how you are going to get it. Give yourself permission to open up, experiment, and see how things unfold. That way, you will not limit the creativity or possibilities that may reveal themselves to you.

Sometimes we cannot see or hear ourselves objectively through our learning process. That is where a personal coach can be helpful, and that's also where I come in. As you coach yourself, imagine that I am sitting on your shoulder, whispering things in your ear, and reading the occasional question bubbles that pop up over your head.

Coaching is always about taking some kind of action. Those actions, however, may surprise you because they may include **being with a feeling** for a while and really experiencing it. It may be **declaring** a commitment or intention. It could also be **reflecting** on a powerful question or inquiry. Whatever it is, it will be to purposefully find what is important for you. We will be looking for what will move you forward and toward the life you want to create—even if you are not sure what that is for you *yet*.

As you coach yourself, take the time to acknowledge your progress, encourage your persistence, and celebrate your breakthroughs. Give yourself the chance to be with these experiences fully before you rush off to the next activity. This is, for many of us, one of the hardest parts of the personal growth process and the one we need most!

Coaching Tip 10

Positively Support Yourself

A Process with Subtle and Profound Effects

Your life is filled with opportunities to learn and grow in extraordinary ways. For the most part, we are so busy *doing* that we have ignored these potential opportunities as distractions and time wasters. Coaching yourself forward from here means that learning needs to become like breathing, continuous and natural, if you want to really reach your personal growth potential and experience an aaah-mazing life.

Just one catch: despite your greatest efforts, you are still going to get stuck at times. While this may seem frustrating, you need to appreciate that the work you are going to do is process work, which is more of a systems-based approach to change. Coaching yourself to be patient will be an important part of *the process*.

This was a tough one for me personally. I have always disliked the concept of process work and wanted action and answers quickly, but I can assure you that this can be magical if you are open and patient. Just like any other practice, such as golf, yoga, or piano playing, the time invested in your process of learning, reflecting, and reapplying adjustments is powerful, and the progress over time is impressive. Trust that when you get stuck, you may need to put in more time and just be patient with the visible, tangible pieces—because internal work reveals itself slowly and in subtle ways, but the impact can be profound. If you are stuck, moving to another area of focus and coming back to it later may serve you well. I do believe that you will figure out some personal sequencing along the way that will guide you as to how you might best break down and break through certain barriers and challenges.

To coach yourself through change and growth, you are going to have to take action—but what that action is could be more variable than you think. We are often expert **doers**, and doing has its place. It allows us to put new behaviors into motion and create forward energy and momentum. Just as often, however, an action that may be appropriate to consider is **being** with a feeling or an emotion or really diving into an experience. We are trying to give further dimension to the learning. Whether this is doing something or being with something, you as coach make the call!

Coaching Tip 11
Coaching Always Involves Action

So, you have *chosen* to be in the driver's seat of your life. You have *taken care of yourself* by fastening your seat belt. In addition, you have ensured that *you are self-sufficiently qualified* to operate at the controls. Now, you need to rely on yourself to drive! This *self-reliance* will be enhanced by building a strong relationship with yourself—yes, building a relationship with yourself! You will now see how *you* are absolutely your greatest resource in this change and growth process. Get ready because through these next few steps, you will be moving **from *driving* to *thriving*** in your selfhood.

Coaching Tip 12

You Are Still Going to Get Stuck …

Coaching is an ongoing process. Sometimes you will do it well, and other times you will not. Expect this. You also need to know that, at times, you will be stuck in a place and will feel like you can't get out. When you are there, you need to understand that you are temporarily **trapped in a perspective.** It is, however, only one of several. We have the ability to adjust our view of our lives from different perspectives all the time. The key is being mindful of when we are stuck and knowing how to move into another place. One technique is to imagine the perspective that someone else would have in this same situation to stimulate an adjustment for us.

Soon,
you will select
an advisory board
to be a resource for you
for times like this. Another
technique to consider using is
physically changing your geography to
stimulate a new perspective. So if you are
feeling down and stuck, go outside for walk or
take a bike ride. Give yourself the encouragement to
mind and mood shift with stimulations you believe
are appropriate for you. **Getting stuck
will happen—staying stuck should
not.** Coach yourself through the
adjustments, and don't forget
to acknowledge yourself
and celebrate when
you do get
unstuck!

*… Be
Prepared
to Adjust*

CHAPTER 4 *aaah!*

Building a Relationship with Yourself

One thing we all look for in relationships is being able to rely on them. Friends and family being there for us is a great comfort—but what about being there for ourselves? What about being **self-reliant?** We know that we have the answers we need inside of us, but do we have the self-reliance to trust ourselves with and act on the truth? This is at the heart of building a relationship with ourselves.

The concept of *aaah!* came to me while sitting by a small river in Costa Rica, just writing and doodling in my journal. I was there with the Omega Institute for an insight and intuition class, and I was committed to spending some quality time alone and getting to know myself better.

Acronyms were not unfamiliar to me; they were tools that I had used throughout my career. But when this particular acronym showed up out of the blue, I knew it was important. A half-hour passed while I was being still by that beautiful flowing water, and the meaning finally came to me: *aaah!* meant awareness, acceptance, alignment, and happiness.

My senses were completely engaged in the surroundings and learning I was experiencing in Costa Rica, and yet throughout the week, I kept coming back to this aaah! acronym. I was looking at it, playing with it, and completely intrigued by it. On my way home, I realized that aaah! needed to have a phrase associated with it. On the plane, the concept of "Open up and say aaah!" was born. At first, it was a cute way to position the aaah! acronym, and it resonated with me, given my health care background. Later, it revealed greater meaning.

Two Important Questions

The concept of building a relationship with yourself may initially seem strange. After all, you probably think that you know yourself better than anyone. You're the  master of your thoughts, you know your likes and dislikes, and you are the one who directs your body to do what it does every day.

Unfortunately, most of us are totally disconnected from ourselves. We live almost exclusively in our heads with our thoughts and do not have the time or inclination to really feel anything. We are literally out of touch, trapped in our routines, and dedicated to the to-do list of the kids, the errands, the house, and the job. Secretly, we hope or even fantasize that an occasional weekend getaway, massage, or night out will rejuvenate us and bring us back to ourselves.

The only way to reconnect with ourselves is to invest time and effort in building this critical relationship. Without this investment, we not only risk sleepwalking through our entire lives but also may miss our chances for being in meaningful relationships with others, including our children and partners. We have an illusion that we are living our lives, but we are only thinking about them, not really having an experience. *Being in relationships with people allows you to experience life, and this begins with our relationship with ourselves.*

The building blocks of this relationship are like those of any other, starting with honesty and trust. The process is also time-consuming and occasionally inconvenient, and it requires ongoing maintenance. However, developing your relationship with yourself, once it is in place, can be one of the most exciting and rewarding experiences you can have. Just wait until you experience how magnificent you are if you haven't already.

The two most important questions to ask as you build a relationship with yourself are:

▶ Who am I?

▶ What do I want to experience in my life?

In this lifetime, we can do many things. We are parents, partners, caregivers, teachers, and leaders—all important roles we play. Still, if we fail to answer these two questions, we will not reach our personal growth potential and have the happiness we really desire, regardless of the many roles we have or the titles we may hold.

We All Have a Story

The biggest obstacle blocking change and growth in our lives is usually our story, that compelling explanation of who we think we are and why certain things have worked out the way they have. We have memorized it and can eloquently recite it to anyone who will listen. The story might include why we have failed at something or why we work somewhere even though we don't like it. It might explain why we have stayed in relationships that aren't good for us. We may list reasons why we have not pursued a particular interest or passion. It is a complete double-album set of sad songs on why others or circumstances have kept us from our success or happiness.

This story holds us in place and keeps us from our own accountability. It allows us to blame or look to others, instead of ourselves, as a cause of our unhappiness. Realistically, we know that we have a role to play in everything concerning our lives and that there are no innocent bystanders. So, in your life, you are the only one who decides to accept accountability to change and grow.

Remember: you are going to have to coach yourself to rewrite that story.

VITAL SIGNS

Family caregivers who provide care 36 or more hours weekly are more likely than non-caregivers to experience symptoms of depression or anxiety. According to a 2002 study published in the American Journal of Public Health, for spouses, the rate is six times higher, and for those caring for a parent, the rate is twice as high.

Source: American Journal of Public Health, 2002

Signs of Vitality

Men are happier than women. Researchers at Princeton University found that, since the 1960s, men have gradually cut back on activities they don't like to do, focusing on working less and relaxing more. Women, however, have replaced housework with paid work and now spend almost as much time as in the past doing things they don't enjoy. Four decades ago, women spent about 23 hours each week doing unpleasant tasks—about 40 minutes more than men. Today, that gap is 90 minutes.

Source: Alan Krueger, Brookings Panel on Economic Activity, 2007

You Need to Reconnect

Understanding your relationship with yourself is a complex matrix of internal and external factors. It involves your:

- Environment—physical surroundings
- Body—the container that houses the person you are
- Health—physical condition and emotional well-being
- Relationships—connections to other people and things
- Feelings—emotions and reactions
- Expression—how you communicate
- Energy and spirit—the essence of who you are
- Mind and attitude—thoughts and ideas
- Dreams and aspirations—the experiences you want in your life

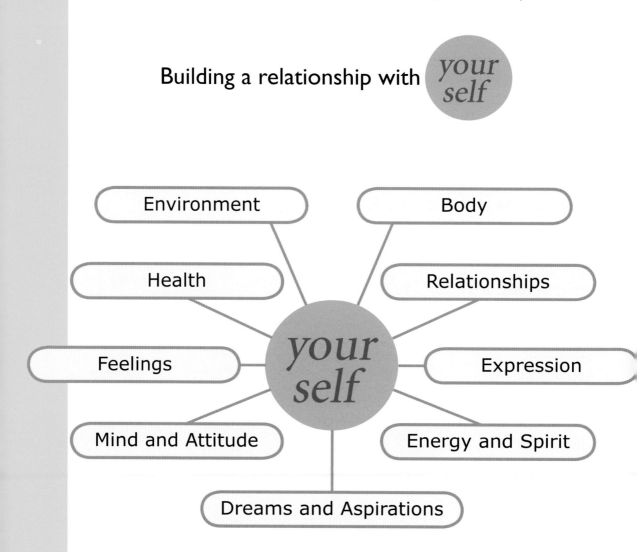

Building a relationship with *your self*

There is a lot to balance, and these elements are intertwined, so it's impossible to deal with one without dealing with many. Your feelings directly affect your energy and spirit, your mind and attitude directly affect your expression, and your overall well-being directly affects your body.

Considering all of this can be challenging, especially when you might be facing a setback or disappointment. Believe it or not, these negative or stressful experiences are actually opportunities. They provide us with **an entry point**, a wake-up call. Maybe your concern right now is getting the test results to a health problem, the information on whether your job is being eliminated, or a call from your realtor about whether your asking price on your house was met by your recent bidders because your retirement savings is counting on it. When we are faced with a change, a life challenge, or a perceived setback, we are given a chance to get greater insight and perspective on our lives and ourselves. Remember that nothing happens by accident and big changes are usually preceded by smaller ways of getting our attention that we may have missed. We may initially be overwhelmed, but in this time and space, we must encourage ourselves to be curious about the circumstances we are faced with and be open to what can be learned here.

The challenge to actually experience our lives more fully is fundamental to building a relationship with ourselves. Life has a full spectrum of emotions associated with it. To cut yourself off from the highs or the lows is to limit your experience. Building a relationship with yourself will require you to expand the breadth and depth of your feelings and emotions. Now this relationship already has the components it needs to be put into effect, and you already have all the answers you need within you. **What you need to do is to *reconnect* with them.**

Some of us may be oblivious to this disconnection within ourselves because we have always been this way. Perhaps in childhood we shut down our feelings because we were told not to cry or to stop complaining. Influential adults may have given us negative messages. In order to protect ourselves as children, we may have needed to disconnect from ourselves emotionally. As a consequence, we have become conditioned to be out of touch with our emotions, and we may avoid expressing what we think and how we feel.

VITAL SIGNS

Caring for others is an increasing occurrence. The Department of Health and Human Services and the National Family Caregivers Association say that more than 50 million people provide care for a chronically ill, disabled, or aged family member or friend during any given year.

Source:
U.S. Department of Health and Human Services, 1998

Signs of Vitality

If you're a caregiver of any other person and you don't take time out for yourself to destress, the results could be devastating. Family caregivers experiencing extreme stress have been shown to age prematurely, taking as much as a decade off of their own lives.
Source: Peter S. Arno, National Caregivers Association, 2006

If we are, in fact, disconnected from ourselves, we need to acknowledge this and start noticing what we may be missing in our lives and what more we can bring into our lives if we do reconnect. Experiences such as love, excitement, challenge, creativity, and passion become possible again when we regain our internal connection and get back to knowing ourselves.

Fortunately, you have many tools at your disposal to do this, including your heart, mind, and voice. Conceptually, you may agree that these sound important, but what does it really mean in the practice of aaah!?

Open Your Mind: Having an open mind is seeing what is possible for you in the bigger picture of life beyond your story that is full of beliefs that may or may not be true. It is about being open to changing your mind about people or things by changing your thoughts and beliefs as you learn and grow. As you listen to your emerging feelings, consciously bring them forward into mindful action. These are the intentional characteristics that define an open mind in the practice of aaah!

Open Your Heart: An open heart means that you are willing to engage in an emotional exchange of both expressing and receiving. For some of us, this may be difficult. We can either express or receive, but being able to work comfortably with both can be a challenge. Opening your heart is also being able to touch others, allowing ourselves to be touched both physically and emotionally, and being connected with our vulnerability and our humanity. When you have an open heart, you are able to endure things that are uncomfortable for you and embrace them rather than avoid them. You are able to accept love, praise, or recognition and celebrate it, not brush it aside because it seems selfish or self-indulgent. Being in a state of emotional flow, both in and out, is the characteristic that best symbolizes having an open heart in the practice of aaah!

Find Your Voice: Finding your voice is about authentic expression. It is integrating your thoughts and feelings, being able to bring them forward in your own unique way. When you find your voice, you take a position on behalf of yourself or an issue and have a compelling point of view you can convey passionately to others. Importantly, you say what you mean and feel, not just what others want you to say or what they want to hear. Keeping things locked up inside of you is unhealthy; asking for what you need and saying what you need to express is healthy. This symbolizes the importance of finding your voice in the practice of aaah!

Of course, we each will have varying proficiencies with respect to our abilities and comfort with opening our minds, opening our hearts, or putting our voices forward. *Wherever you are, this is where you need to be. What is important is your openness to the personal growth opportunities you can have by doing the work ahead.*

From Doing to Being

During my corporate years, I could have been sitting in a restaurant and having dinner with friends in a relaxing environment, and I would have effectively been doing work in my head. My mind would never stop. I would occasionally think about what slowing down would be like, and then I would immediately reject the thought and get right back to doing. This went on for as long as I can remember. I was completely disconnected and clearly had no relationship with myself. And, by the way, this unconscious place was comfortable—that is, until about a year before I left the corporate world. My already complicated world seemed to be getting exponentially more complicated, and where I would usually dive in to fix everything, I was beginning to feel distracted and bored. This was a new experience for me.

While I tried to shake off this feeling and continue, I encountered a road-block or speed bump at every turn. Everything inside of me was slowing down, yet a whirlwind of activity seemed to be raging around me.

Then, I received a message from an unfamiliar place: my heart. It was a call to stop. At first I thought it was a joke. *"Stop what?"* I thought to myself when I heard this soft internal voice within me pipe up.

Just stop.

The message kept coming. For a while, I had been thinking that I needed to move on to other challenges, but I was reluctant, despite both internal and external opportunities. I knew that moving to another company or another assignment was not the answer, and yet staying in place was not going to provide the fulfillment I was after, either. I thought to myself, "I worked hard to get here, a senior executive on a global management team for a major consumer health care company. *Come on! Who just gives that up to stop?"*

The voice would not go away. Each day was a struggle to maintain energy and interest. I was not sure what I would do next, but I did get the message loud and clear. *It was time to just stop.*

From Being to Becoming

I listened to the voice coming from my heart and left my corporate job. My plan was to **just be** and not rush to do for a while and see what happened. Almost immediately, my senses were heightened, and I was feeling and seeing things I had not noticed before. I was fascinated by simple things like the trees, the light and shadows, the sounds of the neighborhood, the hustle and bustle of my town. Even the music to which I was attracted started to change. I found myself interested for the first time in jazz. At first I did not understand why, but then I realized: it was unfamiliar and had no words. In that space with no words or messages, my self-talk started to emerge in a different way. I was noticing more of my inner voice, and it was strong, curious, and confident, even though it did not yet express desires or intentions.

I spent a lot of time writing, journaling, and distilling my observations into insights and learning about what I was feeling. In addition, I engaged in workshops, seminars, and classes as a way to stimulate my ability to give creative voice and description to my personal growth experiences. As my authentic voice emerged in my writing, I embraced it and decided to creatively bring it forward. *Open up and Say aaah!* became my opportunity to express my learning and share with others insights that helped me process the change and growth in my own life. *This book has also been a personal tribute to the relationship I have started to build with myself.*

Delusion, Illusion, and Illumination

Our minds are so quick that sometimes they can outwit us. I had lived so exclusively in my head for most of my life that I can think multiple steps ahead of myself in most situations with ease and comfort. Couple this with a well-trained voice, and I can create delusions and illusions faster than you can say *abracadabra … aaah!*

The external world can seduce us into living out our delusions and illusions. We have the ability to create our experiences in each moment. The problem is that we do it mostly unconsciously and not necessarily in service of our best interests. We either talk ourselves into thinking and believing that our lives are great or are beating ourselves up over how miserable they are. Who would not want our house, our jobs, or our great kids? Or, who would? Yet, if we were more honest with ourselves and connected with our hearts, we would admit that our lives are not that great or that terrible. The truth is that in most cases, life is fine, it is good, and for many of us *good is good enough—for a while*.

What's the problem here? What is it that would create the curiosity and courage to get away from the illusions and delusions and to look for illumination and truth in our lives? Why go after something different if life is already good? Because **you are no longer asleep**. You have gained some awareness through this process, and once you are here, you can't go back.

You are now increasingly curious, so you begin to seek answers.

VITAL SIGNS

In a 2003 study published in the Journal of the American Medical Association, a group of researchers found that a link between the three main Type-A personality traits—impatience, competitiveness, and hostility—increased the long-term risk of developing high blood pressure. The researchers found that both impatience and hostility increased the risk of high blood pressure almost twofold.

Source: Journal of the American Medical Association

Signs of Vitality

Next time you bottle up your feelings, you might want to reconsider. A recent study found that 32 percent of men and 23 percent of women said they typically bottled up their feelings during fights with their partners. While men didn't show any measurable effects in doing so, women who kept their emotions to themselves were four times as likely to die during the 10-year study period as women who always told their husbands how they felt. Being happy or unhappy in the marriage didn't change the risk.

Source: Psychosomatic Medicine, 2007

What you find and how you respond to it will determine the quality of your experience and ***your choice of happiness or happen-ness***. One thing is for sure, though: only you can shine the light on your own life and create illumination. The practice of aaah! can help you chart the path.

The Power of Poetry

Once you have increased your awareness about your life, your mind is vibrating with questions. What does this mean? How do I go forward? For me, however, I knew I was still reasonably disconnected from my heart. You know that true inner voice and quiet knowing place? Some messages had gotten through to me, but I did not yet have a real connection. I had more inside; I just did not know how to access it or whether I was prepared to.

I was already thinking about writing a book but was struggling with organizing it and getting it into chapters instead of a pile of ideas and concepts. My fascination and excitement centered on the change and growth model I was starting to develop.

At dinner one night with a friend, I explained where I was in the process and that I seemed a little stuck. She asked me, "What if it is not a book you are writing?"

I didn't understand what she meant at first. She continued, "What if it was a song or a poem?" "A song or a poem?" I thought. "She is nuts! This is going to be a book!"

My friend was more than just a little intuitive that night. In the back of my mind was my struggle to tap into what I was feeling. I wanted to make a deeper connection with myself, and I believe she sensed that. While the poetry question threw me off guard, I was curious about writing a song because I could see that it would be an emotional and heartfelt exercise. I think she knew that, too.

Intrigued by my friend's question, I went home that night and sat in my bed with my usual pad of paper and pen. In about 10 minutes, I scrawled something down. I was not even sure where it was coming from; it was like automatic pilot, and I was not even thinking. To my surprise, I wrote a poem titled "*I Am You.*"

This was an amazing breakthrough for me in my journey. It was a message from my inner voice to me—a direct communication from that seven-year-old Erica who shut down emotionally years ago. I knew in my mind and in my heart that I was really on my way. You may find that poetry writing is a powerful tool in your journey, as well.

How Your Body Holds Answers

Over the years, I have periodically beaten up my body by eating poorly, burning the candle at both ends, and not exercising regularly. However, I always ultimately regained my focus and motivation to lose weight and get back into shape.

What I now know to be true is that when I am okay with my body, I am okay with a lot in my life. This was such a powerful insight for me, and yet, at times, I would completely disregard it.

Just before leaving my corporate job, I was exercising a lot and was at a good weight and fitness level. I was feeling better about myself physically than ever before, and I was for the first time in my life building strength, both internally on an emotional level and externally in a physical sense. I needed strength to make the hard decisions that were in front of me and to be confident in what I was about to do, and my body really helped to support me with these challenges. In being connected with my body, I was able to keep my mind clear and focused; my energy level was high, and my optimism was strong.

But I'm Not a Poet!

At different points in the experiential exercises, you will be asked to consider writing a poem. Relax—this is not a creative-person-only activity. This is an opportunity to bypass the filter of your brain and to just let your observations of your feelings come through you. Writing poetry can be incredibly liberating, especially for those of us who have little experience or confidence with emotional forms of expression. It is as if you are observing and capturing the emotionally charged feelings objectively without actually having to experience or own them at the time.

Poetry writing is not like journaling, which is more of a cognitive exercise. When writing poetry, you are able to have an emotional connection to your subject, but you take more of an observational perspective when capturing it. Therefore, you are able to express yourself without getting stuck in the emotion about which you are writing. This is why the power of poetry can be so surprising and moving—especially when you read it back to yourself and allow the experience of the emotion to surround you.

After leaving my job, I spent a lot more time working with my body and further building this physical relationship with myself. It became clear to me how much time I had previously spent in negative self-talk about my physical state. As I worked with my body and became more accepting of it, most of that self-talk quieted down, and I realized that I had created more open space in my mind, space that I could now fill with new thoughts and creative ideas.

Finding yoga was a powerful breakthrough for me. Just as I believe all things happen for a reason, *the yoga I chose I believe really chose me*. I found a pamphlet in a retail store. I called for an appointment and signed up for a year membership on the spot. After going twice, I stopped. I did not feel a connection. Not sure yoga was for me after all, I went back to double workouts in the gym and forgot about it for a while. In the back of my mind, it was as if I knew that yoga was going to be important, and I was not ready for it yet. Over the next few months, I thought about it occasionally but was never motivated enough to go back. Six months later, I was suddenly ready. I went to the first class and was hooked. The instructors had changed, and I felt a tremendous connection and chemistry with them. The head instructor, in particular, brought an incredible sense of cultural authenticity to the work we did.

The exercises were hard, but what really captivated me was that we sat together after the sessions as a class, shared tea, and discussed our experiences. This was fascinating to me because it was actually *giving voice* to the

VITAL SIGNS

~ЛлМЛЛ~

Shingles is caused by the virus that causes chicken pox. An intensely painful and potentially dangerous disease, shingles will affect two out of every 10 people during their lifetime, and this year, more than 1 million people will develop the disease.

Source: Novartis Pharmaceuticals, 2007

Signs of Vitality

Moving your body helps—at any age. In 2007, the National Institute on Aging found that, in 30- to 40-year-old adults, regular practice of Tai Chi increased participants' immunity to shingles at the same rate as the vaccine did. Combining Tai Chi with the vaccine produced a 40 percent increase in immunity over the vaccine alone. Of course, the Tai Chi group also reported significant improvements in physical functioning, pain, vitality, and mental health, with a lower rate of depression reported.

Source: National Institutes of Health

physical experiences we were having, which provided incredible learning and insights. The yoga work we did had a heavy emphasis on *energy management.* The energy, once you became more practiced at working with it, literally expressed itself to you. In some cases, the energy communicated through colors, heat, visuals, or physical sensations, but it was always present. Hearing and sharing the different experiences with the class were exciting, and every person and every day were so different. For the first time, I started to *experience* how body, mind, and spirit are interrelated. I also saw how only then was *I was ready for the next step of personal growth, which was the integration of the old me and the new me into the* **now me**.

My most incredible adventure with my yoga practice was a 10-day martial arts learning retreat. It was completely focused on communicating with the body in such a fundamental way that it exponentially accelerated my relationship building. I always knew that my body held messages in it, but it was not until this class that I started to really let go and unlock those messages, release them, and let more of who I was inside come forward without judgment or limitation from the outside world. My biggest breakthroughs were physically experiencing the lessons we try to capture and incorporate into our daily lives on an intellectual level. For example, I learned about the *beauty of balance* when it is achieved, experienced, and demonstrated in the physical sense; the energy, peacefulness, and power of *continuous flow* and *natural movement*; and the flexibility and the impact of small adjustments for unlocking *potential power.*

The Devastating Disappointment(s)

One of the things that can either knock us off track or accelerate our development of self-reliance is what I call "*devastating disappointments.*" We all have them. They are those punched-in-the-stomach experiences you feel when something important to you is ripped away and you realize it's not going to happen or something is thrown upon you that you did not see coming. They challenge your belief system or even your belief in yourself.

How we handle these disappointments and come back from their setbacks, however, says a lot about how strong our relationship is with ourselves and how effectively we manage change in our lives. These challenges open a potential doorway to personal growth *if and when* we decide to walk through it. Sometimes we choose not to. We lock up the disappointment inside of us and carry it around like a backpack. While it's heavy, we believe that it is our baggage to carry. We could choose to learn and grow from it at any time—but this may take us a while to realize. For some of us, it may take years or perhaps the better part of a lifetime.

Whose Dream is it, Anyway?

One of the hardest parts of building a relationship with yourself is that you need to confront yourself on what is true and what is not. You need to clear the air with yourself.

In the corporate world, my personal belief was that you were either striving to be the CEO or you were standing still and falling behind on the fast track. In my personal situation, while I knew I had all the skills necessary for a CEO-level job, I kept sabotaging my own opportunities, as if something inside me knew better than I did consciously.

During my fieldwork time—the year before starting my coaching practice and writing this book—I finally confronted the true ownership of my dream. I had been striving to achieve and prove myself to others my whole life. Finally, I had the opportunity to have the CEO position at a small pharmaceutical company. The dream was here! At that point I was really challenged to step back and think, "Erica, is this what you really want? Is this your dream?" While, intellectually, it still is hard to believe, because so much time and energy in my life had been in pursuit of this goal, the answer was "*No*." A few years earlier, I would not have had the internal strength or determination to make this decision. Instead, I would have let the external pressure of expectations continue to choose for me, as I had my entire career.

I was finally at a point in my life where I did not need external validation to feel successful. My beliefs were realigning, and I was building my own internal expectations for my life. I understood at that point that all I wanted to do was express myself. For a while, my corporate experiences allowed me to indulge in my desire for expression, and in doing so, it fueled my career. But as expressing myself freely became more difficult, I outgrew those circumstances and needed to change. I wanted to be

Erica without constraints and restrictions from the outside world. This was a huge step for me. It was a turning point that allowed me to change the direction of my professional career moving forward.

Until this point, my desires for leadership roles had been mainly as positions for me to hold. Now I was stronger and ready to exercise my true leadership potential through my personal power. I knew I could communicate with, connect with, and inspire people without holding a title and working for a corporation. I was ready to go out in the world on my own, even if I found myself nervous about it at times.

You will know when you have found your dream when you arrive at the intersection of feeling scared to death and feeling excited and compelled to move forward. Without this dynamic edge in your life, you are probably walking a safe path that may be in sight of or parallel with your dream but not likely an embodiment of your dream.

Having explored ways of strengthening our relationship with ourselves, we now have a greater sense of self-reliance. We have started to reconnect to our feelings, our inner voices, and our intuition. The answers inside of us are more accessible, and we are able to lead ourselves from here. Now we need to learn how the elements in the process of change, growth, and happiness relate to each other so we can do our personal work. Once we have these principles in place, you will be *self-empowered* to begin the process of shaping your life on purpose.

VITAL SIGNS

Researchers at Carnegie Mellon University interviewed volunteers over several weeks to get a sense of their moods and emotional styles. Then, they infected them with rhinovirus or an influenza virus and quarantined them. Those who had been determined to be happier were less likely to become ill ,and if they did get sick, they were less likely to complain about it.

Source: Carnegie Mellon University, 2006

Signs of Vitality

A psychologist at the University of Leicester has produced the first-ever "world map of happiness" by using data published by UNESCO, the CIA, the New Economics Foundation, the WHO, the Veenhoven Database, the Latinbarometer, the Afrobarometer, and the UNHDR to create a global projection of subjective well-being. Participants in the various studies were asked questions related to happiness and satisfaction with life. The top-five happiest countries were Denmark, Switzerland, Austria, Iceland, and the Bahamas. The United States ranked twenty-third.

Source: University of Leicester, 2006

Change, Growth and Happiness Connections

We now have a foundation for the elements of selfhood in place. Having looked at taking ownership for our self-care, developing our self-sufficiency through learning to coach ourselves, and establishing self-reliance by building a relationship with ourselves, we can put these pieces into use in the change, growth, and happiness process. By understanding how these parts relate to each other and work in a system, we become self-empowered to effectively use them as we learn to lead and shape our lives on purpose.

If mastering three concepts would give you a road map to happiness, would you want to know what they were? If doing them required that you had to rearrange your preconceptions and take a fresh look at your life, would you still be curious? What if it required daily practice until you were great at it? Would you have the courage to try and the consciousness to stick with it?

While it's unrealistic to think that someone can offer you the five steps or 10 steps to happiness, there are three life skills that can enable you to create your life on your own terms. They are:

1. Be aware of and open to change as opportunity

2. Fuel your personal growth with empowering beliefs

3. Choose the experiences of happiness you want to have

We each have subjective interpretations and personal opinions about what the words "change," "growth," and "happiness" mean. They are loaded words, likely to stimulate emotional reactions, based on our personal experiences. There are, however, dynamics that we can objectively look at as we further shape and evolve our personal beliefs.

Why Is Change So Hard, Anyway?

Change is hard because we believe it will be, so we make it so. Whether initiated by us or from an outside source, change often disrupts our comfort and stimulates a reaction that we usually do not like. If the change is minor, we can usually make a small adjustment and overcome a small inconvenience. However, this type of minor change is not what we fear, is it?

We are concerned with the big changes. We worry about the rock-your-world changes because they have the ability to transform our lives. Serious illness, the death of a loved one, unemployment, a divorce, or an accident can all shake us to our cores. Or, the change could be less devastating but still disruptive, such as moving, taking a new job, retiring, or having a child. These changes make us feel vulnerable and move us into experiences that are new and different. We may not have had a chance to adequately or completely prepare ourselves, so *we are unscripted*. These changes also alter the patterns of our routines and the statuses of our relationships. We may, therefore, be put into positions where we have to rethink things that have become comfortable and familiar to us.

Change can also push a panic button inside of us. It can threaten our **beliefs** that are the governing rules for everything we do in our lives. While our beliefs do create the world according to us, and this may sound serious, *they are simply ideas* in which we place a measure of comfort and confidence. They are projections of what we want to be true, whether positive or negative. What we have to remember is that a belief has no power *unless we give it power*.

We are constantly reinforcing our beliefs and ensuring that we hold them firmly in place. Without them, we perceive that our worlds can be put into a tailspin. Our beliefs anchor us, in both positive and negative ways.

The consequences of changing or letting go of our beliefs can leave us feeling vulnerable, so when they are threatened, we initiate a defense plan. And it will not just be a casual one, will it? No, this is going to be a full-fledged, adrenaline-based, fight-or-flight defense. It is a matter of life and death. Our entire belief system is at stake! This is what we build our world around.

We create resistance to changing our beliefs on a daily basis. Think about the times you express your point of view or take a position on issues. Initially, it's in the context of a civil discussion. Frequently, however, we need to more fervently defend ourselves and escalate our emotional investment. This type of red-in-the-face agitation is what your psyche engages in when it actively resists change. Over time, failure to learn how to navigate change puts pressure on our health and well-being. This resistance will eventually force the critical question we have so far avoided but now must ultimately answer. What do we need to accept and embrace, and what do we need to let go of? In short, what do we need to change?

How Does Change Start?

You've probably heard lots of references to attitude, ranging from "You need to have a positive attitude" to "Attitude is everything."

VITAL SIGNS

Complementary and alternative medicines (CAM) work. The Centers for Disease Control (CDC) and Prevention's 2002 National Health Interview Survey (NHIS) found that deep breathing exercises helped 12 percent of people when used to treat problems such as back or neck pain, colds, joint pain or stiffness, and anxiety or depression, while 43 percent found that prayer for their own health made them better. More than half—55 percent of adults—said they were using CAM because they thought it would be effective, combined with conventional medical treatments. Research is also finding that music has benefits, ranging from managing pain to bettering mood. Stanford University School of Medicine found that depression was reduced when patients listened to familiar music while practicing various stress-reduction techniques.

Source: Centers for Disease Control and Prevention

Signs of Vitality

Positive thinking can increase the efficacy of medicine. When University of Michigan scientists injected salt water into the jaws of healthy young men, causing painful pressure, those who were told that they were also getting a pain reliever experienced less pain. The study showed that their brains also released more endorphins, possibly diminishing the pain of the injection.

Source: Journal of Neuroscience, 2005

aaah! Behavior Drives Attitude

Have you ever tried to lose weight or start an exercise program? I have, and my experiences followed a predictable pattern. First, I would try to get myself psychologically ready for the change by thinking about what I would eat and the exercises I would do. I would do this all morning until it was time to go to lunch or the gym. Then, I would start to rethink my readiness. Should I start today? Or is tomorrow better? My calendar is less busy tomorrow, so I could get to the gym earlier. That would let me work out longer. And this weekend is a big family celebration so I know I am going to cheat on the diet, anyway. It's a better idea to wait until after next week and start fresh. Sound familiar?

These mental gymnastics keep you stuck! What you need to do is decide to take action. Just make a great food choice for lunch or take that 10-minute walk tonight without the whole big attitude-readiness process. That is the heart of behavior change. The behavior choice sends a message to your brain that says, "Hey, did you see that? She just took a 10-minute walk and chose a salad? Wow, she must be serious about this!"

All of a sudden, positive thoughts are being generated in your mind. The change process begins, based on that simple move or action. The thoughts and attitudes will reflect what you do, and you will be on *the road to starting the change process*.

It is incredibly hard to just wake up and decide to have a positive attitude if it conflicts with your belief system. While attitude is certainly important, the first step in the sequence of real and sustainable change is behavior adjustment.

Start to walk and talk like the change you want to make and your attitude will naturally follow. Surprisingly, it will do this from an authentic place because it is taking its cues from your behavior! Change your behavior and you create a new attitude that reflects that behavior—at least for a little while.

How Does Change Get Traction in Your Life?

Initiating change is easy. What's hard is making it stick. This is because making real and lasting changes in our lives affects **an integrated system.** Our beliefs, attitudes, and behaviors are all in lock-step with each other. *The choices we make in the change process have a sequence and a set of consequences.*

This is a good-news, bad-news situation. The bad news is that a behavior-based attitude change can work only temporarily. You haven't yet internalized the new beliefs that go with "walking the talk." So when the first real threat or challenge comes along to pull you out of your new behavior and attitude zone, it's easy to end up back where you started. You were trying out the idea, and it was not yet embodied in your heart and mind. *Game over.*

So how do you sustain change and really get it integrated into your life? You have to work on changing your beliefs! You have beliefs about yourself, your family, your children, your lifestyle, your career, your earnings, etc. You have beliefs about everything. You've gathered them from many sources, including your parents, teachers, communities, institutions, and experiences. Before continuing to accept them just because they have always been there, here are a few questions to ask yourself about these beliefs from your new state of selfhood:

1. Are your current beliefs true for your life right now?

2. Are your current beliefs serving your best interests?

3. Are your current beliefs keeping you stuck or moving you forward?

The only way to create sustainable change in your life is by changing your beliefs—preferably, from self-limiting ones that hold you back and keep you stuck in your old story to expansive ones that create space for you to change and grow into.

How Do We Change Our Belief System?

Beliefs gain and retain their power over time, as we create experiences in our lives that confirm them. We see the world through the eyes of our beliefs. We seek and accept what aligns with them and reject what does not. Eventually, there is nothing to choose or consider: we have our firmly entrenched beliefs, and we will act and behave in accordance with them, whatever they are.

A recent study on stress found that 40 percent of workers reported their job as being very or extremely stressful and 25 percent viewed their jobs as the number-one stressor in their lives.

Source: National Institute of Occupational Safety and Health

Signs of Vitality

Work stress affects more than just your job; it affects your family as well. More than half of actively disengaged employees said that they had three or more days in the past month when work stress caused them to behave poorly with their family and friends. Among engaged employees, the number was only 18 percent.

Source: Gallup Employee Engagement Index, 2003

So a belief can be the magical key that either opens a world of possibility to you or locks you into limitation. It is a key that provides you with entry or passage into whichever world you want to participate. *You have the choice—this is selfhood, after all.*

To get traction in the change process, you create beliefs that support the changes you want to make, and then you actively seek evidence on an ongoing basis to reconfirm them. Take action to learn and discover how those beliefs can be true and then reinforce them in all that you do, say, and experience. Do this over and over again because the more ingrained a belief is, the stronger it is. If you want to be an actor, tell yourself you are one. Go out there and perform in plays. Grab the center stage whenever you can and entertain. Join an acting club and imagine yourself getting roles and parts. Hang out with other actors who have the same interests. Live it and breathe it! You will become it when you believe it.

aaah! Resistance to Happiness Has Consequences

Happiness matters because when we are not happy, not living the life we want, and trapped by our self-limiting beliefs, there are consequences. By denying happiness and our true internal desires, we are creating either active or passive resistance. The outcome of resistance is pressure.

That pressure builds inside of us. At first, it may be slow and may go unnoticed. Ultimately, however, we find that the pressure becomes greater, causing something to blow or break through to get attention. Events that happen to us, big and small, get our attention focused in the right place. If we ignore them for too long, these attention-getting messages start coming toward us with increasing intensity, and we find ourselves with diseases, traumatic experiences, and circumstances that may overwhelm us.

Your belief system establishes the foundations for your attitudes and behaviors. With this in place, you feel grounded and authentic. Pick an empowering and exciting set of beliefs that will stretch you to the edges of your dreams and desires, and then ingrain and practice that belief over and over again to make sure that it sticks. If we choose wisely, we are capable of making our lives just about anything we want!

What is the Connection Between Change and Growth?

Personal growth is the outcome of integrating a positive, new, and sustainable belief into your life. The outcome of a transformative change process is what moves us from places of personal limitation to places of empowerment and possibility.

Think about it. For someone to experience personal growth is a real accomplishment. This person had to consider the challenge of change in his or her life, which means that a personal belief was called into question. He or she needed to have the courage to examine that belief, assess whether it was true for him or her, and determine whether it served his or her best interests. This person then had to make a conscious decision to accept, reject, or modify that belief. As a result, behavior and attitudes needed to be adjusted to now support this new or modified belief. This person also made a conscious commitment to support and reinforce this belief in his or her day-to-day life. As a result, the empowering belief grew stronger and established traction and momentum. Personal growth was the result!

We are constantly being called from within ourselves to live the lives we are meant to live. The challenge is whether we can hear those messages. That internal voice for many of us is incredibly soft. We have not nourished or encouraged it to come forth, so it is often weak, like a muscle that has not been used in a while. And who can blame it for speaking so softly when it is constantly being told by our loud victim consciousness—the saboteur, gremlin, or ego—that it does not deserve to have what it seeks? So we choose to believe that forceful negative voice that limits our view of ourselves, diminishes our sense of courage, and keeps us safe and stuck in our boxes.

We need to access the voice of the true self within us that positively supports our dreams and highest aspirations. While it may be soft-spoken right now, it holds our inner wisdom and knows what is right for us. In our practice of aaah!, we learn how to strengthen this voice of selfhood.

Igniting the dynamics of personal growth in our lives is powerful in that it sets us up to do anything and everything we have always wanted to do. When we view change as an opportunity and have the courage to take it on in our lives, it puts us in a position to choose from enormous possibilities available to us in terms of creating our happiness.

How Does Personal Growth Relate to Happiness?

Personal growth is the result of integrating and sustaining new or modified positive beliefs in our lives—beliefs that move us toward our vision of happiness. By continuing to reinforce and further establish these new beliefs in our process of ongoing personal growth, we begin to more easily and consciously choose the experiences that reinforce them. It's a wonderful cycle. The more we grow, the clearer our vision of happiness is and the easier it is for us to realize that vision. We know what we want, and we believe that we deserve to have it. Our attitude and behaviors support our beliefs. Our next step is choosing the experience we want to have and allowing ourselves to embrace it. This may sound easy, but often we are reluctant to choose.

The choices we need to make include:

1. Will you allow chance or choice to govern the dynamics of your life? This is the happiness versus happen-ness dimension.

2. Will you pursue happiness, or will you settle for being content? This is the creation versus cooperation dimension.

Personal growth is an ongoing process of stretching and expanding who we are into who we are becoming. This mind-set provides us with a continuous chance to challenge and change our beliefs so that they are always empowering us with possibilities.

Consider this: *Happiness is consciously choosing from your possibilities what it is you want to experience in your life and then proceeding forward to live it!*

Read that over a few times and really let it sink in. You must be able to make the choice in order to have the experience. **Happiness is the experience.**

Choosing Happiness vs. Witnessing *Happen-ness*

The difference between happiness and happen-ness is the difference between being a participant and being an observer. Are you in the game, and are you making decisions and choices? Or are you on the sidelines, and are you watching the moves and then providing your commentary on what could have or should have happened? Without personal engagement and choice, we surrender the car keys and take a back seat for the ride, but do we fall asleep and just wake up when we get there? We need to stay alert to the differences between happiness and happen-ness.

Something is always "happen-ing." While observation is important, you need to recognize the difference between being mindfully aware— taking note of what is around you and learning from it—and being a passenger and mindlessly letting things pass you by. Pay attention to what is happening around you and ask yourself questions. What can I learn from this? Is a possibility for personal growth emerging? Consider what is possible, and reflect on the potential outcomes. Then, make a conscious choice about what you will choose to experience next. We are in the state of happen-ness when we allow external factors to make our choices for us, so the choosing is a critical step. By making an active choice in your actions, thoughts, and circumstances, you assume a measure of control over what experience happens next. Happiness is all about personal and active selection of what we want and then allowing ourselves to experience it.

Most of all, don't be intimidated!
If you make a choice you don't like,
you can simply choose again.
We are in a constant state of
gathering information and
experiences. You are
in the accountability
seat for your life.
Don't stop.
Keep choosing.

VITAL SIGNS

The President's Council on Physical Fitness and Sports says that adults 18 and older need 30 minutes of physical activity on five or more days a week to be healthy; children and teens need 60 minutes of activity a day for their health.

Source: President's Council on Physical Fitness, 2008

Signs of Vitality

Positive thoughts help exercisers. Researchers found that those who believed in the health benefits of working out tended to exercise more often, more intensely or for longer periods than those with negative beliefs.

Source: Washington University, 1997

Happiness vs. Contentment

The energy of being happy is different from the energy of being content. In simple terms, one is active, and one is passive, perhaps more politely stated as cooperative.

To be happy requires the energy of continuous pursuit—a choice in this moment, followed by another choice in the next moment. Being happy requires effort to select from possibilities and fully embody the chosen experiences in each moment to really be present in our lives. Some people do it effortlessly, while others require learning and practice.

Contentment, on the other hand, is a passive state of good enough— things are going along well, and there appear to be no tragedies or distractions. We are pleased with our jobs, our relationships, our situations. We are comfortable in our routines, and even if things aren't going all that well, they're bearable. Things are fine. Why rock the boat? We decide to cooperate with fate and let it choose on our behalf. So, cozy in our comfort zones, we coast and assume that everything will remain status quo.

VITAL SIGNS

Income level does not equal level of happiness. A 2006 survey by Princeton University found that those surveyed expected people who earned less than $20,000 per year to be unhappy about 20 percent more than people who earned $100,000 per year, thus reinforcing the perception that the more money you have, the happier you are. In reality, lower earners reported spending only 12 percent more of their time in a bad mood than those who earned more than $100,000. The perception of how unhappy people may be when they earn less was very skewed.

Source: Princeton University

Signs of Vitality

Happy workers enjoy multiple advantages over less happy peers. Researchers at the University of California–Riverside and the University of Illinois found that happy workers had advantages over their less happy peers, according to a 2005 story in the Psychological Bulletin. Happy workers were more likely to land job interviews and be reviewed positively by supervisors. The researchers also found that happy workers are also less likely to suffer from burnout and more likely to have jobs with autonomy, variety, and meaning.

Source: Psychological Bulletin, 2005

This is a choice of allowing life to randomly play itself out at our expense. Change will appear at some point, and perhaps we naively believe we can sleep through it. When change does occur, the question will be, are we ready to embrace it, or will we resist and fight it? The risk of contentment is twofold. First, it lulls us into a lack of preparedness for the opportunities change makes available to us in life. Second, from this state, we are likely to take an unhealthy defensive and resistant stance when reacting to change, which can have negative health consequences.

Happiness is a personal and subjective target. Only you can define it for yourself. Once you define it, you must choose to experience it. It sounds simple, and yet the process to define what we want and how to get there, and then, of course, actually allowing ourselves to choose the experience, is complex. There are lots of places to get stuck along the way.

From Being Able to *Being Willing*

Having a clearer understanding of the dynamics of change, growth, and happiness provides you with the last piece you need to consider yourself ready and able to shape your life on purpose.

The aaah! practice model gives you the opportunity to be willing to take action. The model helps you explore specific areas of your life and overcome where you are stuck. By applying all that you have learned, you can better lead yourself consciously forward and go after what you want to experience in your life.

Let's get into... the practice of... *aaah!*

The Practice of

aaah!

PART

2

CHAPTER 6

The aaah! Diagnostic

The first step in the coaching process is conducting a *discovery session*. This is the time when the coach sits down with the client and asks background questions to learn about what is important in the various areas of that individual's life. Together, they explore goals and priorities and determine what that client wants his or her life to look and feel like. Through this discussion, they begin to shape a mutual understanding on the outcomes and results they will focus on during their coaching sessions and throughout the coaching relationship.

Because you are coaching yourself here—with me, of course, sitting on your shoulder for support and encouragement—you will need an **opportunity for a self-discovery session.**

The aaah! diagnostic is a ***self-directed tool*** that will provide you with this self-discovery information because it is a personalized assessment of how you are managing the change and growth process within a particular area of your life. On the basis of your score, it can also help to *prioritize* where you will want to focus your work in the upcoming exercises.

Remember that the overall goal here is to provide you with insight into how you can choose to experience happiness and well-being more often and in more places in your life. Being able to pinpoint areas that are holding you back compared with areas that are working well for you is an important first step. Typically, we all like to view our results on tests and surveys in the most positive way. Then we typically rationalize our interpretations and focus on areas for improvement where we know we are already strong because it is easier or feels good. Well, here we are going to separate for you the specific areas where you are strong and where you need to spend more time with yourself. You will be encouraged to start where the obstacles are greatest. If you are able to increase the flow of positive energy and change momentum in these spots, you will greatly enhance your overall happiness in this particular area of your life.

Because we are all different, it should come as no surprise that we are each going to have different needs in order to coach ourselves to happiness and well-being. What is valuable in the aaah! diagnostic is the fact that every individual will have a **personal assessment.** That assessment will also vary for the same individual based on the area of his or her life that is examined and the timing of the reflection. For example, if you use the diagnostic on your relationship with your partner now and then again a year from now, you may have significantly different results. *Remember that your self-coaching process will be designed for you and by you, based in large part on the outcome of your diagnostic assessment.*

The diagnostic assessment gives you both a big-picture view and a segmentation view of one area of your life. It will also provide you with directional insights on where specifically you have some blockages or obstacles. Later you will be given exercises on how to move forward to overcome them.

The value gained from the diagnostic is based on a realistic assessment of where you are right now. Be open and honest with yourself. You are no longer a child or young adult who needs to have the "right" answers to the questions because someone is going to judge you. You are in a stage of *selfhood* now. This is all about you checking in with yourself and your life to see how satisfied you are with its progress. There are no right or wrong answers. It is important that you respond naturally and instinctively. Going with the first answer that comes to you is best. If you overthink the question, you are likely to be rationalizing your answers, which dilutes the effectiveness of the diagnostic.

This assessment is designed to force your decision making and choice selection to extremes. You will be asked to select a yes or no response to 45 statements in nine areas. The statements are designed to gain insights into multiple areas that may intersect or overlap with each other. In some cases, the questions may seem to be complicated, and some may even sound similar to each other. Just try to embrace the spirit of the question holistically and answer it honestly. **Remember to focus on only one area of your life at a time throughout the diagnostic**. You may want to consider looking at areas such as your job, a particular relationship, your finances, or your health—but don't feel limited by these examples. You can apply the diagnostic to as many different areas of your life as you wish, but each application should be narrowly focused on one area at a time. Just one note of caution: **do not choose to assess your life in general** with the diagnostic. This is too large and too complex a topic to give you actionable insights.

So go to it... and have... *fun!*

Instructions:

Before starting the diagnostic, please **select one specific area** in your life on which to focus (some examples may include your job, your health, or your relationship with your partner; remember to avoid selecting your life in general, this is too broad an approach). As you respond to the statements, please remain focused on that one area you have selected as your topic throughout the entire diagnostic. You may choose to do the diagnostic several times, each focusing on different areas of your life. Note, however, that the diagnostic is designed to give you perspective and clarity on only one area at a time.

Please review each statement and provide a yes or no response. **If the statement is only partially a yes, please select a no response.** This will provide you with the best results for using the insights of this diagnostic in future exercises and activities.

Part I:

1	I think my environment/current circumstance is completely satisfying, and I am provided with opportunities for achieving my goals and personal growth expectations.	Yes	No
2	I think I am currently interacting with people in this environment/current circumstance who are encouraging and empowering me to be all that I can be.	Yes	No
3	I am completely satisfied with the personal contributions I am presently making and can continue to make, to my environment/current circumstance.	Yes	No
4	I am completely satisfied with the rewards, recognition, and appreciation I am receiving in my environment/current circumstances.	Yes	No
5	I can see my efforts resulting in visible and/or tangible outcomes in this part of my life.	Yes	No

Part II:

1. I think and believe that my overall sense of happiness and well-being is exactly where I want it to be right now. Yes ○ No ○

2. I believe that my moods and feelings are balanced, consistent, and appropriate in most situations, and I do not hold on to unexpressed emotions. Yes ○ No ○

3. I believe that my actions and behaviors are appropriate in most situations, and I do not demonstrate extreme external outbursts of emotions in this part of my life. Yes ○ No ○

4. I feel that all of my needs are being met intellectually, emotionally, physically, and spiritually and that I am completely satisfied with this part of my life. Yes ○ No ○

5. I am deeply satisfied with my life choices and how they are unfolding for me at this time. Yes ○ No ○

Part III:

1. I think I am on track to achieve and successfully materialize the personal expectations I have set for this part of my life. Yes ○ No ○

2. I am pleased with where I am in life relative to where I want to be, and I am personally enjoying the experience and sharing it with others. Yes ○ No ○

3. My life is a living testimony to who I am and what I believe in. Yes ○ No ○

4. I am completely satisfied with how far I have traveled and how much I have accomplished relative to my goals and aspirations in this part of my life. Yes ○ No ○

5. I am personally fulfilled and living out the dream I have in this part of my life. Yes ○ No ○

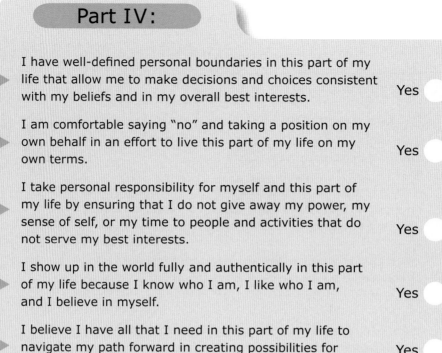

Part IV:

1. I have well-defined personal boundaries in this part of my life that allow me to make decisions and choices consistent with my beliefs and in my overall best interests.

   Yes ⬤　No ⬤

2. I am comfortable saying "no" and taking a position on my own behalf in an effort to live this part of my life on my own terms.

   Yes ⬤　No ⬤

3. I take personal responsibility for myself and this part of my life by ensuring that I do not give away my power, my sense of self, or my time to people and activities that do not serve my best interests.

   Yes ⬤　No ⬤

4. I show up in the world fully and authentically in this part of my life because I know who I am, I like who I am, and I believe in myself.

   Yes ⬤　No ⬤

5. I believe I have all that I need in this part of my life to navigate my path forward in creating possibilities for what is next for me.

   Yes ⬤　No ⬤

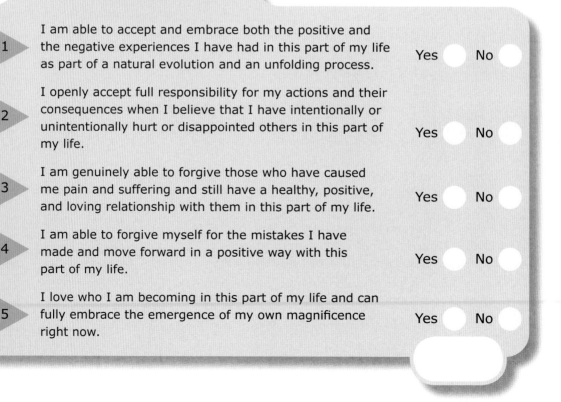

Part V:

1. I am able to accept and embrace both the positive and the negative experiences I have had in this part of my life as part of a natural evolution and an unfolding process.

   Yes ⬤　No ⬤

2. I openly accept full responsibility for my actions and their consequences when I believe that I have intentionally or unintentionally hurt or disappointed others in this part of my life.

   Yes ⬤　No ⬤

3. I am genuinely able to forgive those who have caused me pain and suffering and still have a healthy, positive, and loving relationship with them in this part of my life.

   Yes ⬤　No ⬤

4. I am able to forgive myself for the mistakes I have made and move forward in a positive way with this part of my life.

   Yes ⬤　No ⬤

5. I love who I am becoming in this part of my life and can fully embrace the emergence of my own magnificence right now.

   Yes ⬤　No ⬤

Part VI:

1 ▶ I feel passionate about my desire to grow and make a personal difference in this part of my life, and I do not hold back on bringing forward my gifts and talents to the world.   Yes ◯ No ◯

2 ▶ I believe that my life experiences have brought me purposefully to where I am now and to what I must do now in this part of my life.   Yes ◯ No ◯

3 ▶ I am willing and ready to act on my personal beliefs and to fully express myself in all that I do in this part of my life.   Yes ◯ No ◯

4 ▶ I am looking to participate in and contribute to the world in a meaningful way after having accepted and embraced my role in this part of my life.   Yes ◯ No ◯

5 ▶ I am able to clearly communicate where I have been, where I am now, and where I am going with this part of my life.   Yes ◯ No ◯

Part VII:

1 ▶ I have a clear vision for my future possibilities in this part of my life.   Yes ◯ No ◯

2 ▶ I can communicate confidently about who I want to be and what I want to experience in this part of my life.   Yes ◯ No ◯

3 ▶ I know that I can choose to create and attract any experience that I want into this part of my life.   Yes ◯ No ◯

4 ▶ I am an open-minded person who sees and takes advantage of the opportunities presented to me in this part of my life.   Yes ◯ No ◯

5 ▶ I know what I want in this part of my life, and if I set my mind to achieving it, I will.   Yes ◯ No ◯

Part VIII:

1   I am true to myself and express my feelings authentically in all situations in this part of my life.

Yes ◯   No ◯

2   I am respectfully aware of and embrace my strengths and limitations as pieces of who I am in this part of my life.

Yes ◯   No ◯

3   I believe that I have all that I need within me and around me to create the experiences I desire to have in this part of my life.

Yes ◯   No ◯

4   I feel that I am whole in this part of my life. I have successfully integrated pieces of the old me with pieces of the new me and am fully living and expressing myself in the now me role.

Yes ◯   No ◯

5   Because I have ensured that all of my personal needs are being met, I am energized in this part of my life and can enjoy giving to others my attention, love, and gifts.

Yes ◯   No ◯

Part IX:

1   I know that I am fully embodying and living "out loud" the life that I was meant to live in this area.

Yes ◯   No ◯

2   I have a clear purpose for this part of my life, and I am experiencing it in an integrated and authentic way.

Yes ◯   No ◯

3   I know that each experience I have is a guided message to keep me moving forward on my path for the fulfillment of my purpose in this part of my life.

Yes ◯   No ◯

4   I am clear on what happiness means for me. I allow myself to consciously choose to experience it and express it in this part of my life in every way I can.

Yes ◯   No ◯

5   I am moving in the flow of this part of my life and experiencing trust, freedom of expression, and abundance in all that I do.

Yes ◯   No ◯

Scoring the Diagnostic

After you have completed the diagnostic, please use the following scoring system to determine your results:

 If you answered yes to ALL of the statements in a section, give yourself a **CIRCLE** score

 If you answered with 3 or 4 yes responses in a section, give yourself a **TRIANGLE** score

 If you answered with 0 to 2 yes responses in a section, give yourself a **SQUARE** score

You should have nine shape scores, one for each of the sections of this diagnostic.

Now you are ready to **transfer your shape scores** to the scorecard on the next page to complete your personalized profile for where you are currently with respect to growth and change in the chosen area of your life.

What do the shapes mean, and where do we go from here?

Each shape represents a state of **readiness** for embracing the challenges of personal growth and change you have in the particular area of your life. As we go through a brief description, you will see how you may be closer to or further removed from your personal desire, or **happiness target**.

Your *aaah!* Diagnostic Scorecard

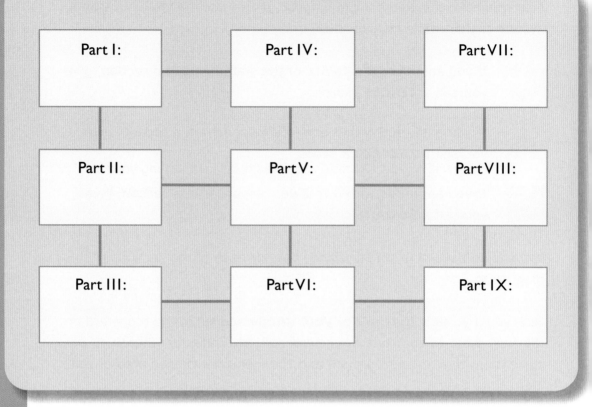

Example of a completed scorecard:

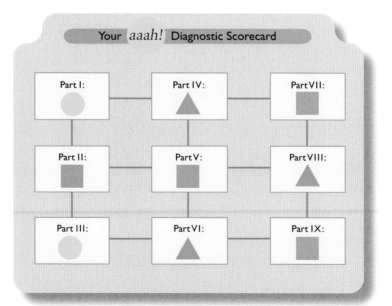

Your Personal Geometry

So, now you should have a board filled with some combination of squares, triangles, and circles. What does this personal geometry mean?

The Square: A square is an indication that you currently have several self-limiting beliefs about certain aspects of your life in this area. This may be causing you to feel stuck and may result in you not fully living the life you want.

External or internal circumstances may be inhibiting your ability to achieve your goals and aspirations. You may be unhappy in your current job and may dream of doing something else but feel trapped by financial concerns. Perhaps relationship challenges or tight finances are sapping your energy. You may be **boxed in** by your own beliefs and may not have the necessary sense of readiness to claim your dreams with conviction. Regardless of why the square is there, it's great that you've honestly identified its existence. That's the first step to moving beyond those limitations and moving toward the realization of your dreams.

The Triangle: A triangle means that you are open to making some adjustments or have already made some in this area of your life but you still have a few self-limiting beliefs that are holding you back from what you ultimately want. The good news is that you are **trying some different angles**, so you also have some empowering beliefs that you are trying to use in this part of your life. You are in a state of flux, with a mix of positive and negative influences. Spending some time addressing your challenges here could open you up to greater possibilities of personal growth and happiness in this area of your life.

The Circle: A circle means that you likely feel centered, grounded, and strong in this particular area of your life. You have embraced who you are and what you need here. Your challenge is to continue to feed the strength of and nourishment for this area to help you maintain your positive outlook and grow even more confident and magnificent in this area of your life. It can even perhaps be an area where you can now give back, having achieved some mastery in this part of your life. Remember, however, that change and growth evolve in a circulinear way, so stay close to these areas and continue to work on your continued happiness and well-being. You are **standing in the circle of your personal truth** and are on your way to achieving your dreams. Can you grow and make your circle even bigger? This is your question *now!*

Interpreting the Overall Results

Your results are not good or bad. If you have a bunch of squares on your chart, **don't** allow the voices of your ego or saboteur to start telling you that you are screwed up, just as you thought you were. For those of you doing a celebration dance because of your circles, **relax.** And for those of you who have already started to justify that your triangles are really not that bad after all, **stop.** These conditioned reactions and judgments are not necessary or helpful. What you need to do now is take a step back, breathe deeply, and get ready to "Open up and say aaah!" This is your road map for the journey forward. *You are exactly where you need to be, and the only thing that is important is what you choose to do next.*

So, What Is Next?

I am now going to introduce you to the "Open up and say aaah!" practice model. As we go through it, you will see how the model works and what each of the boxes means so you can put your shape scores into perspective.

CHAPTER 7

Building and Understanding the *aaah!* Model

Developing the concept of aaah! into a model was not my original intention. Yet, I am not surprised that this is exactly what resulted. I have always appreciated when information was *framed with both context and perspective* so I could see the overall picture of where I was and where I was going. Here, you will now be able to see how your tic-tac-toe board of shapes translates into a **framework of information and insights**. The model will provide you with an easy-to-understand structure for gaining clarity on where you are in your personal change and growth process. It will be your road map as you coach yourself forward.

We All Need a Personal GPS System

Technology enables us to be connected to each other everywhere, every minute—and yet, there is no technology that we can plug into and use to connect with ourselves. Many of us perhaps need to experience the extremes of tension and external disruptions so we can willingly call ourselves back to our deep-rooted desire of reconnecting emotionally and feeling again. It is a big challenge, given the external stimuli to which we are exposed.

We certainly have every chance to avoid ourselves because:

- We live in a point-and-click world of computers
- Instant messaging has created a new language of abbreviation
- Writing skills are a vanishing art in the world of e-mail communication
- On-demand digital technology allows us to watch and listen to anything any time
- We are addicted to e-mail, the Internet, cell phones, PDAs, and voicemail
- We work longer hours and have less face-to-face contact
- We are global citizens operating on a 24/7/365 clock
- The Internet is always on

We are in constant motion to the point of exhaustion, and we self-medicate this with yet another cup of coffee. It may be a strategy, but it isn't healthy. In my coaching practice, I frequently find that I need to encourage my clients to slow down. To internally find the answers they are looking for, they must allow themselves to "be with" an experience or feeling, more than they need to immediately leap into action. While action is a necessary ingredient for any type of change and growth to occur, the definition of action is often only one-dimensional. In coaching, action is as much about being engaged emotionally and feeling something as it is about physically doing something. Knowing when to choose each will become second nature to you.

Think about the GPS system in your car. If you don't take that right or left turn when it directs you, it recalculates your route. Similarly, as you process new signals from your body and mind, your internal guidance system will recalculate the route forward from where you are now and will give you new instructions. *The sophisticated wireless internal hardware of your instincts, intuition, and emotional guidance system is always there to course correct you through the process.* Trust that you know where you are going and how you need to get there. The model can provide you with a big-picture view and a segmented view of what the landscape looks like, but how you work through it will need to be decided and personalized by you.

If you let it, this process will unfold for you exactly as you need to experience it.

Trust yourself.

The Model Is Holistic and Surrounds You

We are integrated beings. As much as we like to separate our lives into pieces and segments, we are one within ourselves. Sometimes we try to compartmentalize the various aspects of our lives for the purpose of short-term focus and sanity. It is troubling, though, when we allow permanent walls to be built in select areas because that disconnects us from our center, our essence. We begin to operate as one person in one environment and a completely different person in another. Of course, we all need to adapt ourselves to various situations to function in the world, but, for example, if your job violates your core beliefs or if you're miserable in your home life and trying to act happy when you're around other people, that serious disconnect will inhibit your personal growth.

For a while, we can maintain this disconnect and possibly even be functional. Over time, however, it doesn't work. *Happiness is an integrated experience.* In order to fully embody it, we must live our lives with integrity. For most of us, this means living in accordance with our dreams, values, and personal priorities. Some people may feel that this is too self-indulgent—that we must put the needs of others ahead of our own. So, we put off our dreams and goals until the kids are grown, until the money is saved, or until retirement. The problem with that is your life is meant to be lived now, every day, and in each moment. There is no stopping and waiting—we have only now. No one else can make our lives what we want them to be. Listen to your internal GPS system, your inner wisdom.

The *aaah!* Model is Circulinear

Like most things in life, the model will also be circulinear for you. You may feel like you've gotten one of the phases of the model right, only to find that you have lost ground in another area. Don't let this upset or discourage you. Remember that as you work with yourself and reconnect, you are working through a dynamic change process of **breaking down** and **breaking through** old paradigms and belief systems and creating new ones. There is no right and no wrong here. You will make progress; you may also relapse to old thoughts and patterns. Don't worry! This is normal. What is most important is how quickly you recover from a setback and get back to work with yourself. Know that you are going to make mistakes, have setbacks, and get stuck. That is life. What makes this process transformational is the persistent and consistent ability to be aware of when things are off track, accept what has happened, and get yourself back into alignment with your goals and objectives as quickly as possible.

Traction and Momentum Build Commitment

To be successful in anything, our forward movement must be grounded in and directed by fundamental principles. Armed with these and the knowledge of what we wish to achieve, we can gain traction in the direction we are heading.

Traction is the concept of digging in and making forward progress. It is the difference between rugged tires that effectively grip the road and carry us over the most challenging terrains and weak, worn tires that spin endlessly, causing us to slip all over the place. With traction, we are not spinning our wheels endlessly, lost and confused. We have a hold on the foundation we are working on, and we dig into the information enough to grasp it with confidence and feel it with our hearts and in our minds.

Traction allows us to gain momentum, a **self-propelling** dynamic in which we accelerate our progress by aligning energy with purpose. When our flow of energy is working with us, our aligned thoughts and feelings allow us to create the possibilities and experiences we want in our lives. The aaah! model is going to help you get traction and establish momentum in the areas of your life that you wish to change. You will be establishing confidence and commitment to keep going and keep growing.

Learning Styles: Visual, Auditory, and Kinesthetic

Adult learners have different styles by which they absorb and process information. Many people prefer to see things, others prefer to hear things, and some learn best through touch or experiencing their learning directly. We all have one dominant style and use another quite often, usually with one of the three being our less favorite way to take in information.

I am a visual learner. I always have a pen in my hand and draw pictures to illustrate my emerging thoughts. Others may prefer to physically experience or try out what they are learning: they are first to pick up the box on the table or touch the fabric in a store. These are kinesthetic learners. The auditory learners like to read or listen for their preferred intake. What is important, as it relates to learning styles, is acknowledging that people vary in their preferences and that the best way to ensure that messages are being absorbed by all is by offering the learning through a variety of techniques. In celebration of my visual preferences, you will experience an extensive pictorial display of how the model and the diagnostic work. You will also read (which is a form of hearing) the explanations for each section. Last, the "Tools and Treasures" sections will give you opportunities to touch and feel some of these concepts as you engage in the various experiential learning techniques. While you will have preferences for some of the exercises, challenge yourself to engage in a sampling of everything and *notice for yourself what type of learner you are.* This will be valuable information for you as you continue on your personalized journey.

Linear and Conceptual ... the Power of AND

Intentionally or not, we are constantly putting the people around us in labeled boxes. We may describe them as empathetic or analytical.

Someone may be a linear thinker—able to analyze details but not very strategic. Someone else might be wonderfully creative but unable to balance a checkbook. Think about some of the boxes you use to define people. What are the boxes that others use to define you? Are you analytical or creative? Are you introverted or extroverted? Are you the intellectual or athletic type? We all have preferences, just as we noted above for learning styles, and we are all capable of being two things at once and not as limited as some would like to think.

One of the challenges in using this model is allowing yourself to experience it in both a linear and a conceptual way. Some of you believe there is a specific order for doing everything. Others believe you can start anywhere and get it all done eventually. Here, you don't have to follow a set of rules. In fact, when the model is built in front of you, it will be done in a conceptual way. When it is described in detail to you, it will be done in a linear way.

Either way, go with it and learn something. What is most important is that you make connections and see the relationships between each of the parts. Whether you work with the model in a sequential piece-by-piece way or in a big-picture way, both are fine. Don't get locked into reading the model only horizontally or only vertically. Experience it as a whole. It is fluid—just like life.

This Is a Safe Space for You to Experiment

One of the hardest things we face when trying to change and grow is finding a safe place to do it. The external world can be full of pressure and judgment. Our friends and family have points of view on everything we do, as well as a vested interest in keeping us boxed into certain beliefs and behaviors for their comfort.

Finding an environment where you feel free to try out some new ideas and some new ways of being may be tough. This is why many of us seek out coaches and therapists to help us navigate through challenge and change. After all, there is nothing like having a dedicated champion who stands in our corner, cheers us on, and helps us to find our way forward on our way to **selfhood**.

Still, we may not be ready for that step, or we may have tried that step and it did not yield the results we wanted. Now you have the opportunity to define that safe space for yourself, with me on your shoulder and your soon-to-be-named advisory team on call and ready to step in with encouraging perspectives. So really let loose and play here. There is no right or wrong answer in *selfhood*—try different activities and beliefs to determine whether they are aligned with the core of who you are. Then, you adopt some, discard others, and learn from all of them. Will you choose to swing with all of your might, trying to hit the ball out of the park with a personal breakthrough? Or will you stand in a ready position, just watching the pitches that come over the plate as you are frozen in a half-ready stance? No one is watching.

Take your Swing.

Interpreting Your Diagnostic— Shaping Your Life on Purpose

You have a general knowledge of what each shape means, but what is it that will move you along the continuum so that you can bust out of your squares, round the edges off of your triangles, and step into your circles? This is where your journey really begins. This is where you can now play, practice, and participate in **shaping your life on purpose**.

You are the keeper of the lines. These shapes represent how you are choosing to draw your lines around you. Are you rigid, defined, disappointed, and stuck? You may not be surprised that you have a square in this area. Are you trying different options, adjusting, caught between a rock and a hard place, pleased with some things, and still disappointed with others? You may have a triangle in this area of your life. Are you excited, energized, making an impact and a difference, learning, and growing every day? This sounds like a circle.

Moving from one shape to another is not magical. It is an outcome of building a relationship with yourself, practicing some critical skills, and declaring an intent to live well and be happy. *The practice of aaah! is intuitive and natural; it is also forgiving.* If you get off track and catch yourself back in some of your old limiting places or patterns, take a deep breath and congratulate yourself for your skills of awareness. Without it, you would not have noticed that you were off track. Once you catch yourself, ask what it is that you need to accept in this moment to move on. Refocus on what it is that will move you along the continuum so that you can get out of your squares, through your triangles, and into the circles.

Middle of the Road Could Be Collapsed Extremes

We are all conditioned to see and believe what we wish about ourselves. One or two positive things in an otherwise unsatisfying life can create an opportunity for us to weave an illusional or delusional story of happiness.

In forcing you to make choices in the diagnostic questions, the model identifies and isolates specific focus areas in each phase of growth and change. Your personalized diagnostic assessment is *designed to separate* different areas that you may otherwise collapse into one, which creates a distorted view.

A good analogy of how this works happened to me when I was in the corporate world. I was a general manager for a consumer health care division in Toronto. We were looking at the mediocre business performance of a major brand. I knew the brand had two main lines and asked the team to separate them for evaluation. What we found was that one line was on fire from a growth perspective, and the other was terribly underperforming. When examined in aggregate, everything looked just slightly below average, but that wasn't what was happening at all.

The same lesson can be applied within ourselves. Breaking the bigger pieces into smaller pieces will let us see where challenges are so that we can pinpoint some exercises for growth. In each stage of the model, you will get a look at three distinct areas, and you will get both a big-picture view and a close-in view of what is and is not working.

You will also need to look closely at your triangles in your diagnostic. It will be important to assess whether the triangle you received is really about positive movements you are making in several areas simultaneously and they are just not solidified and in place yet or whether you have some collapsed beliefs on the extremes of empowering (circles) and disempowering (squares) and they are generating the score of a triangle. So let's stay alert to this and make sure we are working the right issue.

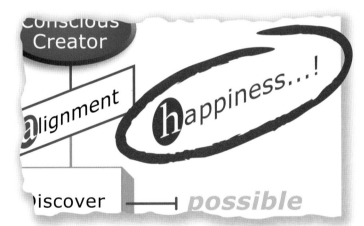

Expectations and Attachments

Throughout this journey, you should remind yourself to stay focused on the *what*. What do you want in your life? The *how* should be flexible. We all have expectations. What gets in our way of happiness is when we get attached to those expectations and limit the creative, natural process of life unfolding as it is meant to rather than as we have predetermined it to be. Relax and trust that this will unfold for you exactly as it is meant to be. You will find your way through this. You choose how you experience what happens in your life.

Putting the Model Together Piece by Piece

The model is now going to be built for you piece by piece. As we go through it, I will explain how it all fits together so that you are comfortable with the dynamic and flow. On a conceptual level, the model has **six pieces**.

Piece 1: Happiness!

The overall purpose for the practice of aaah!—and specifically the *h!* in aaah!—is to experience the happiness we want in our lives. Happiness is our goal, and all of the steps and actions we take will be in service of this. You will always see the aaah! acronym with an exclamation point after the *h!* This is in recognition of the fact that when we choose to go after our happiness, we are taking a strong position on behalf of ourselves. However, this position is not without controversy, conflict, or a host of other dynamics with the external environment or our internal negative voices, right? Remember that we must have courage in going after our own definitions of happiness. You should be proud of your pursuit to claim and experience yours!

Piece 2:
Three Stages and Three Skills That Empower Them

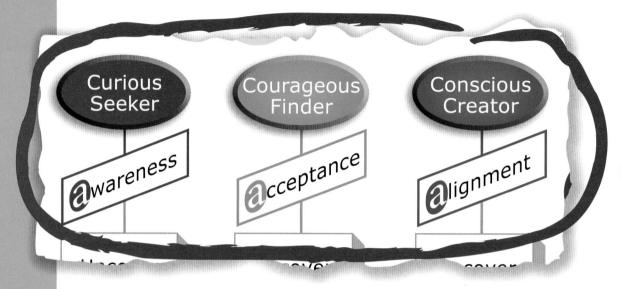

The second piece of the model highlights two important things. First, it introduces the three stages of growth and change we will be traveling through. These phases are the **Curious Seeker**, the **Courageous Finder**, and the **Conscious Creator**.

Second, it completes the definition of our *aaah!* acronym by identifying the critical skills we will be discussing and using in our process. These are specifically *(a)wareness*, *(a)cceptance*, and *(a)lignment*. As you can see by the layout, each of the three phases of growth and change is empowered by one of the three critical skills in aaah!

Piece 3: The Goals and the Questions

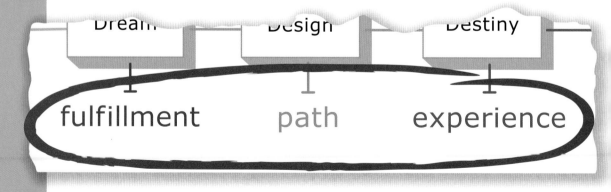

The third piece of the model reveals what the goals are for each of the three stages of change and growth. The Curious Seeker is in search of **fulfillment**. The key question in this phase is "*What do I want in this area of my life?*" The Courageous Finder is in search of **the path**, driven by the question "*How will I design the way forward?*" The Conscious Creator is in search of **the experience**. The key question here is "*What will having the happiness I desire feel like and be like?*"

Between pieces 2 and 3 of the model, we can see how the vertical axis (down the model) is laid out and how it works. Let's now take a look at the horizontal axis (across the model).

Pieces 4 and 5:
Aligning Yourself to Look Outside, Inside, and Around

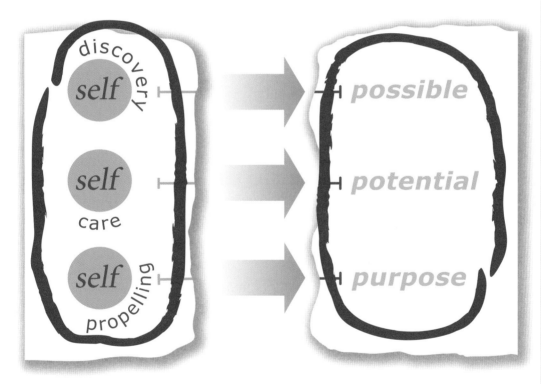

In piece 4 of the model, three perspectives will help you take a closer look at yourself across the three stages of growth and change. While you are looking at how to **move yourself forward** from these different vantage points, you will be given a sense of what your target is in piece 5.

Self-discovery: This perspective begins with looking at our life as an objective, outside observer and noticing our **environment.** If we were to select two words that describe self-discovery, they would be "**see it**." From this view, you are looking at what is here now. You are a mindful observer from this perspective. You are noticing things all around you, perhaps things you have not noticed before, things that may have always been there but that strike you just a little bit differently now. From the self-discovery perspective, your focus is on identifying the **possibilities** that can exist for you in the environment of this part of your life.

Self-care: This perspective takes us more deeply into our own feelings, beliefs, and **internal view of our world.** Again, if we were to select two words to describe this, they would be "**feel it**." From this view, you are digging deeper into your heart and are finding out what needs to be resolved within yourself and your belief system so that you can, in fact, reach your full **potential** in this area of your life. Our potential is what we can be in our lives without limitations. On our way to realizing this, we must face, deal with, and process the baggage and distractions that we have closed ourselves off to and have potentially chosen to ignore. We need to manage ourselves through the change and growth process while being mindful of both our health and our happiness, given their connectivity. This will require that we bring our integrated selves forward and that we are *right* with ourselves from the inside, which can result in challenging work in terms of changing our self-limiting beliefs.

Self-propelling: This perspective of viewing the world considers our personal relationship with our **mission in life.** The two words that would describe this area are "**be it**." From this view, we are focused on our movement toward and embodiment of those things for which we have passion. We can all create for ourselves a vision of what happiness looks and feels like in a particular area of life. In propelling ourselves forward, we are in search of our **purpose** for that desired experience, with the end result being our authentic and integrated true selves.

Piece 6: *The Boxes*

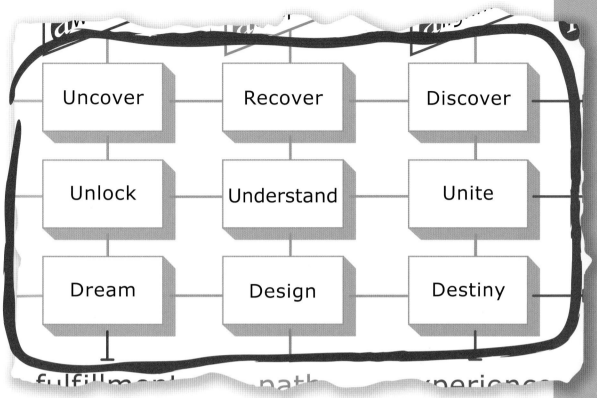

This section of the model contains nine boxes, three each for the three stages of change and growth, providing rich areas for personal exploration. The diagnostic assessment you completed provided you with insights for each of these boxes. Your squares, triangles, and circles reflect your personal satisfaction with managing change and growth in each of these areas.

Choosing an Advisory Team

We all need support, perspective, and advice. But this is a self-coaching practice, and in many ways what brought you here was the attraction of the possibility to work through some of your issues/questions on your own. Well, no worries. You will create a **virtual team** of advisors who will work with you. Some of them are familiar to you, and others might be new, but either way, you are assured of getting some great perspective.

Here is how it works: on the next page there is a chart and at the back of this book is a perforated card for you to detach. Both contain a graphic for you to use to name several members of your virtual advisory team. What will be interesting is that these individuals will be able to advise you, but they will be powered by your own voice and the relationships you have or can imagine having with them. These people can be friends, acquaintances, people you don't even know but admire; they can be dead or alive, real or fictional.

You need to select eight people according to some specific criteria:

MENTORS
Select two people who represent strong, rational advisors, people who have made tough decisions in their lives and who have been direct and honest. They have sized up the opportunities and were able to put the emotional issues aside in service of the best decision for the issue at hand. The only requirement is that you believe you have a strong sense of how they operate and would trust and follow their opinions if they gave them to you. Some examples could be Oprah Winfrey, Warren Buffet, your father, or your best friend.

Buddies
Select two people whom you just love and want to have on your advisory team because you can! No requirements— you just intuitively appreciate them and think they would be fun to have on your team!

HEROES!
Select two people who each have a strong presence and voice that you admire. They have a way of communicating in a persuasive and clear way. They captivate your attention, and you admire their charismatic and authentic voices. Some examples may include Jack Welch/a corporate CEO, Tony Robbins, Ronald Regan, your high school sports coach, your favorite nonfiction author, or your favorite newscaster.

SUPPORTERS
Select two people who have a heart-based approach to life and who you believe can compassionately understand you. They can relate to your feelings, are gentle, and would be able to hold your best interests in a loving way as they offered you advice. Some examples may include your God/your higher source, your mother, your partner, your puppy, your child, or your best friend.

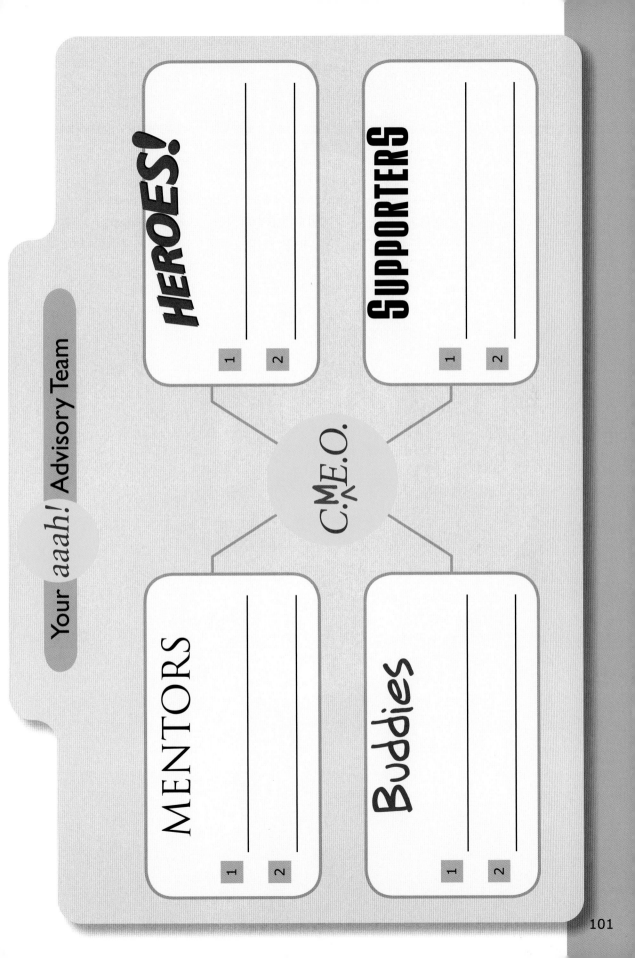

HEROES!

1
2

SUPPORTERS

1
2

C.M.E.O.

MENTORS

1
2

Buddies

1
2

The Big Picture

Next, you will see the completed model with all of the pieces and stages identified. In each of the sections that follow, we will explore in great detail the three stages of the change and growth process as you learn how to develop your personalized practice of aaah!

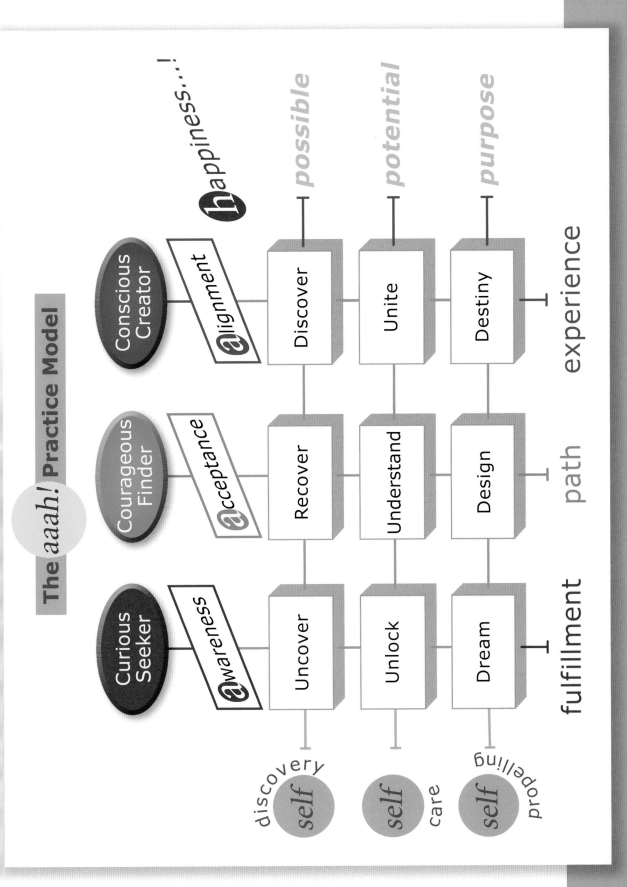

The *aaah!* Practice Model

The *aaah!* Practice Model

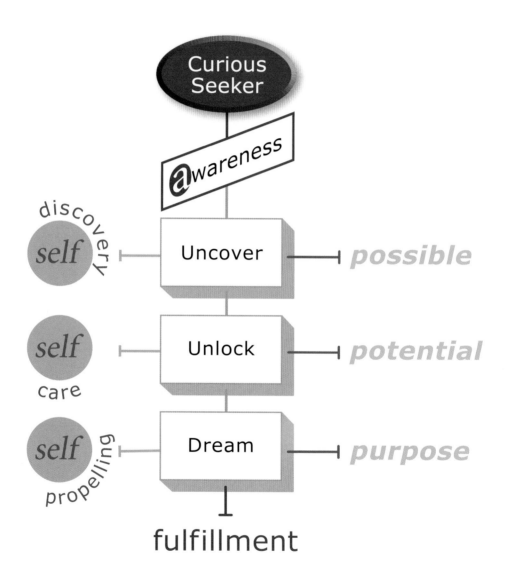

Curious Seeker

@wareness

self discovery — Uncover — possible

self care — Unlock — potential

self propelling — Dream — purpose

fulfillment

CHAPTER

8 aaah!

The Curious Seeker

You can be anywhere, doing anything. Either suddenly or gradually, you realize that you have a heightened awareness about what's going on around you. You feel like an observer of a movie in which you are starring. You find yourself drawn to situations with a desire to investigate or learn, and your mind wanders as you try to figure out exactly what you are feeling.

You are in search of something but are not quite sure what. Something is different, though. You feel grounded, yet something is nudging you, poking at you. You are intrigued. The feeling follows you for days or, perhaps, weeks. You know that the feeling is not going away and that it wants you to notice it. Finally, you stop and pay attention to it. How could you not? You realize that, no, there's nothing wrong with you. *You've simply had your first brush with being a Curious Seeker.*

Greeting the Interfaces

The Curious Seeker is the *first of three phases* along your journey of managing change and growth. It can be described as becoming alert and awake in your life in a new way. Your routine is interrupted, and you are acutely aware of things that look and feel different, even though they are familiar to you. Has this rug always been this color? Was this chair always here? Why is this annoying me today? Is this what I have worked my whole life for? Will this routine ever change? The Curious Seeker is beginning to look at the world through a new lens and is questioning some fundamental things about his or her life. *Somewhere, somehow, a line has been crossed.*

The questions can start anywhere, but they usually begin with observations about your environment. Your emotional sensitivity begins to increase as well. You might think, "I have heard that person say that a million times, and it never bothered me before, but now it makes me angry." Initially, the Curious Seeker may try to shrug the whole thing off, but the observations and feelings continue to come. While some will choose to rationalize this awakening and sensitization as nonsense and will throw themselves back into their daily grind, others cannot. They follow the trail of these new observations and feelings that have broken through, wanting to know more about where they came from and what they could mean. Aaah! ... the true Curious Seeker emerges.

The Curious Seeker craves rationale and insight about what is going on. He or she starts looking for information and connections to satisfy this craving—there is a clear sense that changes are on the horizon.

We already know that change can be stimulated in our lives by many things. For the growth process to start, however, we need an entry point. Without a point in which to gain a foothold, change and the possibility for growth appear as blips on our radar screens, generalized disturbances that either cause havoc or ultimately go away, at least for a while. For the Curious Seeker who is awake and alert, however, this is a breakthrough message. It is an opportunity to **greet the interfaces**—a chance to acknowledge that outside of you, inside of you, or around you, something has broken through to your consciousness. But what does it mean, and what should you do next?

One of the most fascinating things I have learned about coaching is that we really have all the answers inside of us, without exception. Why, then, are we so often confused and frustrated with our lives? *The simple truth is that we need the right questions to bring out our answers.*

Below the conscious surface of the Curious Seeker is someone who is not totally fulfilled in a part of his or her life. He or she may be content, highly functional, and going through the motions of everyday life, but something is missing: life is just not being lived the way it was originally intended. So, what is going on *within* the Curious Seeker?

Questions the Curious Seeker is pondering usually include:

1. Is this all there is?

2. What do I really want?

3. Is this the dream I had for this part of my life?

These are questions many of us face and often torture ourselves with at some point in time. Most of us feel afraid of or can't deal with the gravity of them, so we ignore them and hope they will go away. The Curious Seeker, however, is ready to go to work. *It is time.*

The Target for the Curious Seeker

You will recall from the aaah! model that the Curious Seeker is *looking for fulfillment.* Fulfillment is not, by the way, a straightforward or easy target to hit.

To be fulfilled is to be living in accordance with your values, beliefs, and aspirations. It is an internally guided direction that completely satisfies your deepest personal desires without concerns about external judgments. *It is for you, by you, and in service of you*. It is the work you love regardless of money or title, the lifestyle of simply being you without question, or the partnership that is just right. Sounds great? Like a fantasy or dream? *All of this is attainable*.

Fulfillment is both a *being state and becoming state,* not an endpoint or a destination. It is an ongoing process of making conscious choices about what we want, regardless of challenge, difficulty, or criticism from the outside world. It is also about how we show up in the world as we pursue what we want. Getting to fulfillment often requires facing some hard truths and taking difficult positions on behalf of ourselves. I have even heard it described as being a *radical act*. Let's take a look at what is involved in pursuing our fulfillment.

Critical Skill Building: Awareness

A phrase you often hear before someone is ready to make a change is "*awareness is the first step*." Getting to a point of being aware that change is necessary is not easy. Developments have already been under way in your subconscious. In your personal journey, **awareness is the entry point** to the conscious process of change. Without awareness, we cannot intentionally or purposefully progress in personal growth. When we are ready to acknowledge and embrace awareness and go where it leads us, we are off to a good start in the change and growth process.

Awareness is the primary tool of the Curious Seeker who is now awake, alert, and at attention. Focusing that attention is the next step.

Curious Seekers are aware of an increasing desire building within them and are driven to satisfy it. In their search, they become aware of **interfaces** in their lives, places where they come into conscious contact with a boundary, or a connection point, they previously did not see. Curious Seekers can often hold a perspective of viewing themselves as separate from the other side of the boundary and can objectively observe and explore it from a point of detachment—thus, our phrase of "greeting the interface" because we are so acutely aware of its presence. This stage of change and growth has three interfaces. Each holds important learning and insight.

As a Curious Seeker, *your environment* becomes the first major interface for you to notice clearly. It is either supporting or not supporting your quest for fulfillment. You are also becoming more aware of your *internal emotional interface,* which includes personal beliefs and feelings. Here, too, you begin to recognize that your beliefs either empower your wants and desires for happiness in your life or they hold you back.

You will become aware of a *relative interface* that also begins to emerge. This considers the fact that things aren't always absolute and specific or exactly as they appear on the surface. We must open ourselves up to the concept of having a *relative perspective* and be able to get at the essence of what may have been *intended or implied* by something. For example, reflect on a dream or desire you may have had in childhood or early adulthood. Your ultimate experience may have been different from the original view, but the essence is perhaps the same. I know that for me personally, my childhood dream of being a doctor absolutely was not realized, but my professional coaching, writing, and speaking career is focused on the relative essence of *helping people be better*.

The skill of awareness building can take a while to activate within us, but once ignited, it accelerates, with no turning back. It is, in effect, letting your genie out of its bottle. If you choose to embrace the energy of awareness, it will lead you forward. *Choose to ignore it and it will cause you greater angst now that you have questions that need answers.*

Our ability to use our awareness skills has important outcomes:

1. *We get clarity on what we see and feel as well as what surrounds us.* Awareness allows us to receive insightful messages as we consciously engage with our environment and surrounding circumstances.

2. *It wipes away the "delusions" we have created.* We have all fantasized about what we wish to have in our lives. Awareness erases delusion and brings the revelation of *"what is really here now."* Only from here can we begin to move forward.

Get Clear with Yourself

Let's put our awareness skills to work as we explore the pieces that make up the Curious Seeker stage. These are the **Uncover, Unlock, and Dream** boxes in the model. As you engage with them, you will be given questions to reflect on and exercises to experience. You are going to invest time in learning about yourself so you can shape change and growth in your life on purpose. Later, you will also commit to actions you are willing to take that will help you pursue your fulfillment goals so you can experience the happiness you seek.

aaah!-wareness Coaching Tip

Let's try some exercises to build up our observation and awareness skills. This will help you be present within your surroundings and within yourself.

1. Each morning for the next week, set an intention about what you will look for today in your environment. For example, you can focus your attention on noticing people, colors, or structures (furniture, buildings, etc.). In the evening, make a short journal entry about what you observed. Notice whether you found yourself more alert and noticing things that jumped out at you. This may seem simple, but building up your awareness "muscles" will take a little practice.

2. Expect that messages will come to you today, and every day this week, that will help you learn about yourself. Notice who shows up and what they say. Be curious and receptive to the messages. Note how you feel. Be alert to the music you hear. Which songs catch your attention, and what emotions do they stir up? Write a short journal entry each day about your observations and feelings.

3. Act as if each day this week, your entire day is being filmed or voice recorded. Notice what you are caught on tape saying to people. Do you commonly use certain words or phrases? Are you listening and responding to the questions asked of you with thoughtfulness and originality, or are you reacting with well-rehearsed answers? Are you hypnotized in your environment, or are you engaged and responding to what you are experiencing in real time? Write a short journal entry with observations about your behavior. Are you surprised by anything?

The ability to nurture the skill of awareness is important. Once comfortable using it, we can call on it at any time to give us greater clarity in any situation. *Awareness is the critical first skill to master in our pursuit of change, growth, and happiness.* It is the powerful first piece of the *aaah!* acronym.

The Uncover Box

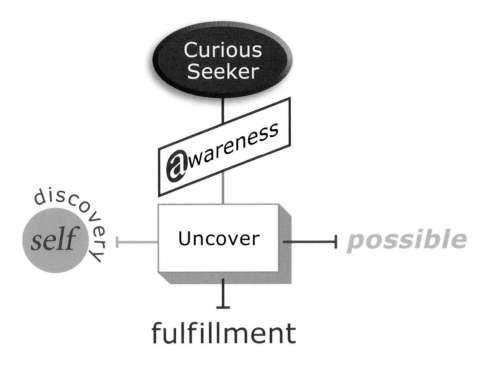

The Uncover box is first within the Curious Seeker phase. The focus here is **your environment,** the interface between you and your external circumstances. On the basis of your diagnostic assessment, this could be your workplace, your home, or some other environment. To reconnect and start building that relationship with yourself, you need to begin the **self-discovery** process of observing and noticing your surroundings. What is here now, and what is **possible** for you in this environment? This is your first entry point to consider in the change and growth process.

Visualize your selected environment in your mind. Try to *feel* what it is like to be there. Is it bright, inviting, and generally attractive? Do you notice people having fun and being positively engaged in what they are doing? Or, is it a place that feels dark and uninviting? Do you observe people who are stressed, frustrated, or unhappy? Notice what you are seeing and sensing in your surroundings. Remain somewhat detached right now and treat the exercise as if you are watching a movie.

The purpose of the Uncover box is to gain awareness and clarity about *the energy your environment currently holds*. If you believe it is a positive and encouraging place, you are likely to have scored a circle in your diagnostic. If it is a mix of experiences—things you like and things you don't like—you may have scored a triangle. If this place is neutral or negative for you and limits your self-expression or opportunities for reward and recognition, you are likely to have scored a square.

What is important here is that you begin to see how your diagnostic score relates to your experiences. For each score, including the circle, you can take actions to move you further forward in the change and growth process.

Rememb-aaah! Stay Focused on Fulfillment!

Acknowledging the truth may be hard, but either your environment is empowering you to fully be, express, and experience your desires or it is inhibiting you. You may love where you are and the people around you, but if the rewards and recognition are not enough for you, you will not be able to have the impact you want to have with your life. This is a common situation. We are comfortable in our surroundings, so we convince ourselves that we do not need certain things, and we begin to settle. Or, we begin to rationalize to ourselves that we are too needy and that other people are too busy to notice our contributions. We convince ourselves that everything is fine. Oh, except just one thing: *this environment does not fulfill you!* You want to be fulfilled, and if there are missing elements for you, this is a call to action. This is your point of entry in the change process. Do you want to exist and just get by? Or do you want to live the life you have always dreamed of? Tough choice? The Curious Seeker wants more. **Don't settle!**

aaah-mazing Questions?

For each box, you will be given 10 aaah-mazing questions to consider. If your score is a **square** or a **triangle**, try to spend some quality time with these questions. If your score is a **circle,** consider reviewing these questions to uncover deeper learning and insight. The questions are designed to engage you in reflection about a particular area of your life. They also strengthen the critical skills for their phases. For example, each of the boxes in the Curious Seeker stage will have questions directed at increasing your awareness as you search for fulfillment.

Some questions you will be able to answer off the top of your head. Others are mid- to longer-term reflective questions you may work on over a few days or even a few weeks to gain meaningful perspective. This is an *ongoing learning process* for you, so give yourself some space and time here. The most significant outcome of this journey is in building a relationship with yourself and coaching yourself through the change and growth process. If you find that some of the questions do not resonate with you, skip them and focus on those that do. **Feel free to be selective**.

For those of you looking for *deeper exploration*, consider pondering these questions in your meditation or prayer practice, through journaling, or in the creative processes of drawing, painting, or developing a vision board with words and pictures. *All of these approaches involve different senses and experiences to surround you with your answers and provide* **illumination, reflection,** *and* **expressive** *insights.*

As you consider these questions, stay focused on the life area on which you focused during the diagnostic. This is the beginning of the process of working through those shapes in your personalized assessment.

10 aaah-mazing

Uncover Box

Questions?

1. When do you think most about your environment (morning, throughout the day, bedtime)? Notice the times and frequency. How would you characterize your thoughts (negative or positive)? How can you improve your environment and your experience there?

2. How does your environment inspire you?

3. Which personal values are fulfilled in your environment? Not fulfilled?

4. How can your personal growth be unleashed here?

5. What can be asked of you or said to you to ignite your energy and enthusiasm here?

6. How has your impact in this environment been satisfying and positive for you?

7. What lie are you telling yourself that is keeping you stuck in a story about your environment?

8. What truthful expression or perspective, if you put it forth to others whom you share this environment with, would start to rewrite your story?

9. Which one behavior, if modified, would send a strong positive signal of change and momentum to your environment?

10. What belief must you change in order to sustain this behavior in question 9?

aaah! The Value of Tools and Treasures

Remember that the **tools** are the *experiential exercises* and the **treasures** are the *lost pieces of you* that you will find along the way.

This is why the "Tools and Treasures" sections are so important to the process of building a relationship with yourself. Please know that these exercises are not going to provide you with the detailed answers to solve your specific problems or challenges and that the change and growth process is not an overnight phenomenon. *So don't get frustrated—get playful.*

They will stimulate your senses, get you thinking out of your entrenched perspective where you see things only one way, and provoke a *childlike creativity* within you to help you to express yourself more openly. *The exercises also directly relate to the "Open up and say aaah!" approach of using your* **heart, mind***, and* **voice** *as guides*. All of the exercises will be asking you to illuminate (see with your mind), reflect (feel with your heart), or express (voice through words, pictures, or physical positions) yourself. Remember that all of your answers are within you and they need to be stimulated with  provocative questions and exercises. Each section will use a blend of techniques so that visual, auditory, and kinesthetic preferences can be accommodated.

Tools and Treasures

If you have a square or triangle in the **Uncover box**, your environment is not fully supporting your desired or best interests right now. This could be a subtle or dramatic experience for you. It may require making a change to remove you from it or a modification to make it more appealing to you and effective for you. Your goal is to objectively assess it and see what you can gain from increasing your awareness through these exercises. A change in perspective can open up new possibilities and considerations, or it can confirm a need for action. Be guided by the intellectual, emotional, and intuitive messages you gain from these exercises as you search for your fulfillment.

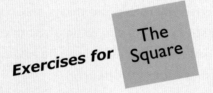

Exercises for The Square

Illumination
What positive and negative messages do you consistently receive from your environment? Make a short list of them.

Reflection
Which scene best describes your environment metaphorically: ocean, forest, or desert? Write a brief description of how your environment is like this part of nature.

Expression
Choose a body language position (yes, actually get up and move) to describe your environment. How does it feel to be in this position? Write a few words about this.

Exercises for The Triangle

Illumination

With an imaginary camera, capture a picture of the best memory you experienced in this environment. Write a brief description. Now capture your most memorable disappointment or frustration here. Write a brief description.

Reflection

What specific and tangible changes (in your control), if made to your environment, would dramatically change your experience here? Write a two- to three-word description of each.

Expression

Which musical instrument would others claim reflects their experience of you in this environment? What is their message to you here? Which instrument do you believe best reflects who you are in the environment? What is your message that you want to convey? List the instruments and messages.

Exercises for The Circle

Illumination

Imagine that a great book of learning contains all that you want to know about this environment. What would be your title for this book? Make a note of it.

Reflection

Behind your front door is someone you have always wanted to meet in this environment. Who is it? What message does he or she have for you? Write a few thoughts.

Expression

You have been sent flowers to congratulate you on an accomplishment in this part of your life. What is the message on the card, and whom is it from? Write a few words.

uncover box

A Plan of Action for the Uncover Box

Having completed the exercises recommended by your shape score or perhaps even venturing beyond and doing more, you have had a chance to expand your current views about this area of your life. Maybe you creatively explored some new perspectives that were stimulated. You may now see your challenges and opportunities in new ways, all of which helps to reconnect you to yourself.

We will specifically take the learning from these experiential exercises as well as your answers from the aaah-mazing questions and put them into actions you can take to move yourself toward your fulfillment goals, or **happiness targets**, as we call them in the practice of aaah! Now let's put some achievable next steps in place to create some traction and momentum in your change and growth process! *Here is where the coach within you gets to step up!*

Take a few minutes to review your answers to the aaah-mazing questions and your responses to the experiential exercises. Consider thoughtfully, with an open heart, what messages are embedded there for you to notice. What is calling out for you to see, feel, and express with regard to this area of your life? You can still go back and explore additional exercises in the "Tools and Treasures" sections for other shapes if you crave more learning. This is your chance to capture your internal insights into where you are and where you want to be going.

You will now be given a chance to map out an action plan where you will shape this part of your life in a new way.

Here is how it works:

Happiness Blockers (HB)

Identify the three obstacles (physical or emotional) you believe you have in this particular area of your life. Use your answers from the questions and exercises as information sources for you. Be specific and clear about what is holding you back in this part of your life. Write them in the spaces on the action plan page.

Happiness Insights (HI)

Again, on the basis of your answers to the questions, the experiential exercises, and your internal vision of what happiness looks like for you in this part of your life, identify three new pieces of learning or insights about your environment that you did not see or consider in this way before. Write them in the spaces on the action plan page.

Happiness Target (HT)

Here is where it all comes together in terms of committing to the changes you will now make to realize your personal growth and experience the happiness you want in this part of your life.

Using your happiness blockers (obstacles you see) and happiness insights (opportunities you see) as guides, you are going to define three actions you can take that will be a commitment to you moving toward what you want in this area of your life. Your happiness target should be a specific action you can control and accomplish.

It should both be meaningful and have a high probability of successful implementation because it has been developed with consideration of your obstacles and opportunities. Make sure that each of the three goals or happiness targets is an **expansive** and **empowering commitment** for you. You are in a state of *selfhood* and are seeking your fulfillment in life. *Your goals should be exciting enough to strive for!*

Coaching yourself here is all about encouraging your boldness, your bigness, and your openness to possibilities. You have all that you need. The answers are within you, and the tools are all here to help you once you have selected what you want. Get your happiness targets out there in your world by setting a clear intention to experience them. By doing so, you will take the first step toward creating your happiness!

The *aaah!* Action Plan

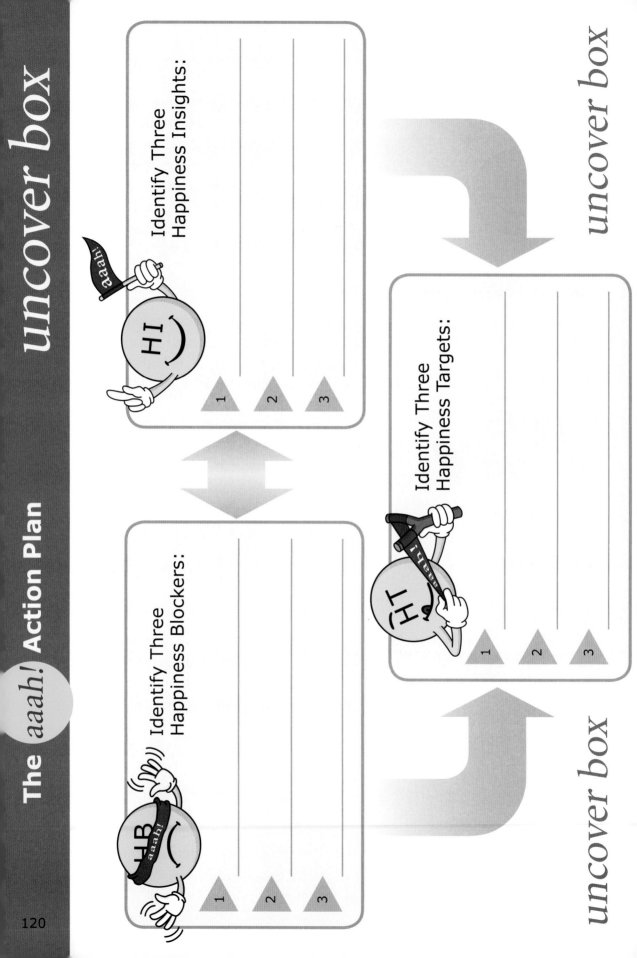

Identify Three
Happiness Insights:

1
2
3

Identify Three
Happiness Blockers:

1
2
3

Identify Three
Happiness Targets:

1
2
3

The Unlock Box

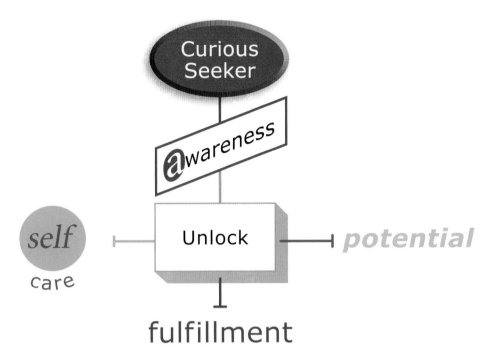

Now that you have taken a look at your external environment, let's go deeper into our Curious Seeker journey and take a look inside ourselves by exploring the Unlock box. The *interface we greet now includes our personal beliefs and feelings.* Here we become aware of whether our current beliefs are empowering us to experience what we want or holding us back in self-limiting patterns. Emotionally, we need to be honest with ourselves. Are we fulfilled and happy? Or are we are angry and frustrated, holding onto disruptive or unexpressed negative emotions below our surface of exterior control?

When was the last time you stopped and allowed yourself to notice how you were feeling? It might be something simple, such as feeling energized after you exercised or feeling satisfied after a great meal and a glass of wine. Or, perhaps it was something more complex, such as feeling sad when you said goodbye to your kids as you left on a business trip.

When you get in your car to run an errand or walk into a conference room for a meeting, what do you notice about how you feel? Are you anxious, angry, or excited? Do you breathe deeply with comfort, or do you notice a fast-paced shallow breathing, indicating you are stressed? What is the conversation that is going on in your head? Are you encouraging yourself and feeling confident about how well prepared you are? Or are you beating yourself up again for taking on too much, along with a dose of "and why does this all matter, anyway?" as you reach for a cookie to make you *feel* better?

As we move into the second box of the Curious Seeker stage, we enter an emotional realm. Here we will explore our feelings about our fulfillment in this area of our lives and which emotions we are expressing or holding onto. Part of our **self-care process** is appropriately expressing our feelings so we don't create stressful resistance that can cause health consequences. So let's explore this box and see what **potential within** you can be further unlocked as we bring awareness to it.

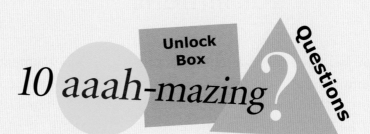

Unlock Box
10 aaah-mazing **?** Questions

Remember to stay focused on the area of your life
for which you completed your diagnostic.

1. Make a list of the emotions that you crave to express but that you have not allowed yourself to experience. What has been holding you back here?

2. Around which emotion are you most likely to have a negative outburst? Anger, frustration, sadness? A positive outburst? Joy, humor?

3. Which of the following four areas, if improved, would dramatically increase satisfaction in this part of your life: intellectual, spiritual, physical, or emotional? How would you improve them?

4. Consider what authentic expression would look and feel like for you here if you were able to be open and honest about your fears, needs, and desires. On a scale of 1 to 10, where 10 is you're already there and 1 is it seems like you'll never get there, how close are you now?

5. What does it feel like to be balanced and in control of your emotions in this part of your life? On a scale of 1 to 10, how close are you now?

6. How comfortable are you in your ability to communicate with others in an open and expressive way emotionally? How effective are you in doing this on a scale of 1 to 10?

7. When you have experienced a negative emotional outburst, how long is your personal recovery time (minutes, hours, days)?

8. What is your most touching memory in this area of your life that inspires you to now take a positive step forward toward your goals and aspirations?

9. Recall the last time you asked someone for emotional comfort. What was the experience like to ask? What did you receive? How did it feel?

10. What is your emotional self-talk in this area of your life? Are you positive or are you beating yourself up? Are you beating up others silently inside yourself?

Tools and Treasures

Exercises for **The Square**

Illumination

List 10 things for which you are grateful in this part of your life.

Reflection

Recall how your parents modeled emotions. Do you express yourself similarly or differently? Are you pleased with this? Write a few words that capture your feelings.

Expression

Pick two people on your advisory team and ask them to write—through you, of course—a description of their impressions of you as a person. Consider exposing a side of you that may not be as familiar or visible to others or even yourself.

Exercises for **The Triangle**

Illumination

An important child in your life is concerned about you. Write a letter to that child about why you are excited about your future in this part of your life so he or she does not need to worry.

Reflection

Remember a time, in this area of your life, when everything was working well and you felt great. What were you doing, who were you with, and what feelings did you experience? Write a few words to capture this.

Expression

Imagine that all your doubts, disappointments, insecurities, and frustrations are each represented by a rock you carry around in a backpack. Each day before leaving your house, you put on this backpack that holds all the negative emotions you have collected in this part of your life. Now imagine going to a lake with your backpack. Take out each rock one at a time and briefly acknowledge the feeling it represents. Toss it into the water. Do this for all of the rocks. Did you see any patterns develop? What is this experience like for you? Write a few words capturing your feelings.

Exercises for **The Circle**

Illumination

Imagine you are a light bulb that has three levels of brightness. You are currently at level two. What does level three feel like for you? What can being brighter in this part of your life mean for you? Write a few words that capture this.

Reflection

Ask two members of your advisory team to challenge you to experience something ridiculously big and completely out of reach for you—but something that reflects your deepest desires in this part of your life. What do they ask you to do? What in these challenges is appealing to you? Write about the feelings you have.

Expression

What does expanding boundaries of emotional expression look like for you (for example, giving a passionate keynote speech or singing in a church)? Write a few words.

unlock box

aaah!

A Plan of Action for the Unlock Box

It's time again to make our action plan. ***For greater detail, please refer to the Uncover box instructions.***

Review your answers to the aaah-mazing questions and your responses to the experiential exercises. Now with a quiet mind and an open heart, work through your happiness blockers, your happiness insights, and the action plan as indicated below.

Happiness Blockers (HB)

Identify the three major obstacles, physical or emotional, that you have in this particular area of your life. Write them in the spaces on the action plan page.

Happiness Insights (HI)

On the basis of your answers to the questions, the experiential exercises, and your vision of happiness, identify three happiness insights that demonstrate your learning about what your personal potential is in this part of your life. Write them in the spaces on the action plan page.

Happiness Target (HT)

Now define three actions you can take that will be a commitment to moving toward fulfillment in this area of your life. Make them things that you can control and accomplish—and exciting enough to strive for!

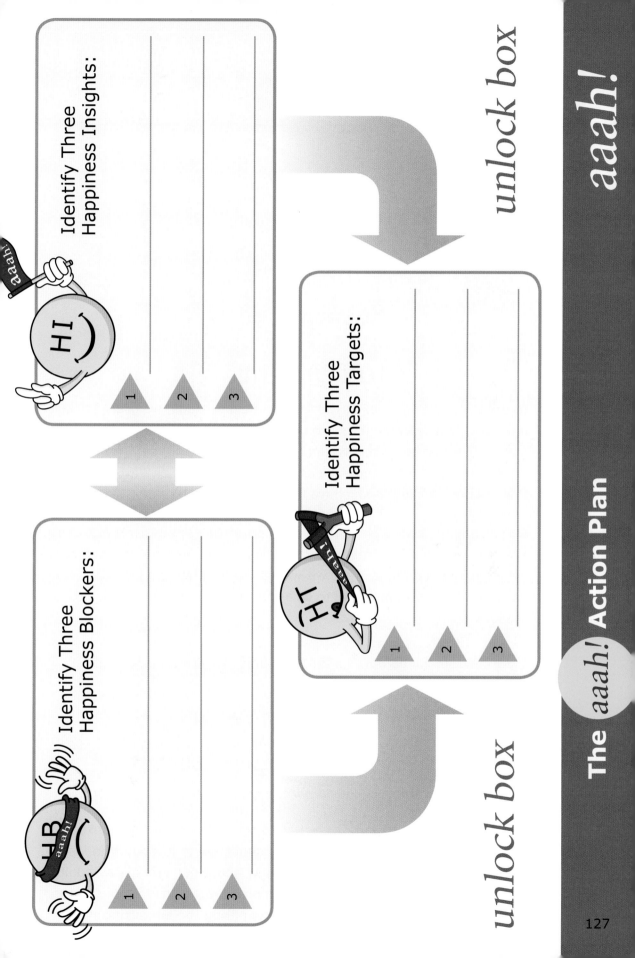

Identify Three Happiness Insights:

1
2
3

Identify Three Happiness Blockers:

1
2
3

Identify Three Happiness Targets:

1
2
3

unlock box

unlock box

aaah!

The *aaah!* Action Plan

127

The Dream Box

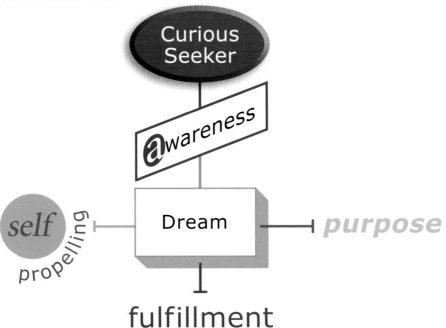

In the third and final box of the Curious Seeker stage, *we greet the last interface, that between ourselves and our mission in a particular area of our life*. The last box is the Dream box. It represents our **self-propelling** drive to find and experience the *essence of our dream* or our **purpose** in this area of our life for which we have potentially lost sight.

Do you have a dream? Many people, surprisingly, say no to this question. I believe we all have a dream and a purpose in this lifetime. In childhood, we were inspired about what we wanted to be when we grew up. Why were our dreams so powerful to us as children? I believe there are three reasons:

1. We imagined how it would *feel* and what it would *be* like.

2. We chose it for ourselves! It was ours, it was not imposed on us, and it could not be taken away.

3. We intuitively connected to it from a deep inner knowing place.

Sound familiar? An early version of the practice of aaah! *at work.*

This dream begins to fade as we grow up and become hypnotized by daily life. We lose track of it, lose our connection to it, and often lose a bit of ourselves with it. When asked now about our dreams as adults, our responses range from projecting impressive visions for our futures, to claiming to be living the dream, to admitting the embarrassment or defeat of not having a dream. None of these states is satisfying. To live a happy and fulfilling life, we have to genuinely reconnect to the essence of our original dream. In childhood, we expressed a role we wanted to play. What about being that doctor or firefighter is the essence of its attraction? Is it problem solving, care giving, or adventure? Let's try to get back in touch with the essence of our dream.

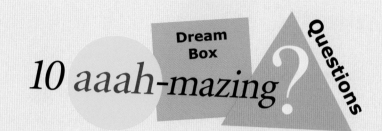

10 *aaah*-mazing Dream Box Questions

Remember to stay focused on the area of your life
for which you completed your diagnostic.

1. When you were a kid, what was a great day like for you?

2. Who was your best friend, and what did you like to do together?

3. What did your parents or adult role models encourage in you?

4. What gifts and talents emerged for you in childhood?

5. Where and how are you using these gifts and talents in your life now?

6. Which part of you are you most excited about sharing with others every day?

7. As a child, were you free and easy or serious and focused? As an adult? What changed?

8. What is it about you that you know is unique? How do you know?

9. What do you internally sense or know to be your purpose is in this lifetime?

10. What dream or expectation did your parents have for you when you were a kid? How did you follow it or ignore it? What dream or expectation did you have for yourself? How did you follow it or ignore it?

Tools and Treasures

Exercises for The Square

Illumination

You are your *future self* (imagine it is 10 years from now), and you are speaking to college students about the importance of finding and following their dreams. What insights can you share based on your personal learning? Write the highlights of your speech.

Reflection

You have only 24 hours left on earth. You are given total physical health and presence of mind for one day to experience your dream. You can make three telephone calls to set up your experience. Who do you call, and what do you ask for? What is the dream? Make a few notes.

Expression

What is the dialogue you have with your God/source/ universal energy/higher self regarding your dreams and aspirations? What specifically do you ask for? Write a few words about this.

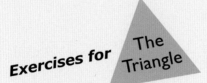

Exercises for The Triangle

Illumination

You are cooking (imagine this even if you never enter the kitchen). What is the dish you prepare that represents your true expression of your dream for yourself in this lifetime? Write your dish's name and what it says about you.

Reflection

What are the three most significant pieces of feedback you have ever received about how you have affected the lives of others? Capture it in a few words.

Expression

What is the body language expression you have for living your dream? Select one word to describe it. What is the body language expression of never living your dream? Select one word to describe it. Create an inspirational phrase that encourages you to go after your dream. Write it down.

Exercises for **The Circle**

Illumination

You have a radioactive quality about you. Whatever you touch, you leave behind an essence of who you are. Describe it in a few words. Go ahead—brag!

Reflection

You are addressing a group of peers who look up to you. You are asked to share your philosophy on managing change to achieve personal growth and happiness. What words of wisdom can you offer from your experiences? Write your advice.

Expression

What *personal currency* makes you feel wealthy? Is it when people say "I love you" or give you hugs, smiles, or kisses? Is it humor? Choose something that captures you. Write how it feels to give and receive using this currency.

dream box

aaah!

A Plan of Action for the Dream Box

Please refer to the Uncover box action plan for more detailed instructions on how to proceed.

On the basis of your answers to the aaah-mazing questions and your responses to the experiential exercises, you will now develop an action plan for forward movement.

Happiness Blockers (HB)

Identify the three major obstacles (physical or emotional) you have in this particular area of your life. Write them in the spaces on the action plan page.

Happiness Insights (HI)

On the basis of your answers to the aaah-mazing questions, the experiential exercises, and what you know about yourself, identify three happiness insights that demonstrate your learning and drive about what is propelling you forward in search of your dream and toward your purpose in this area of your life. Write them in the spaces on the action plan page.

Happiness Targets (HT)

Now define three actions you can take that will be a commitment to you moving toward your fulfillment in this area of your life. Make them things you can control and accomplish. Make them exciting enough to strive for!

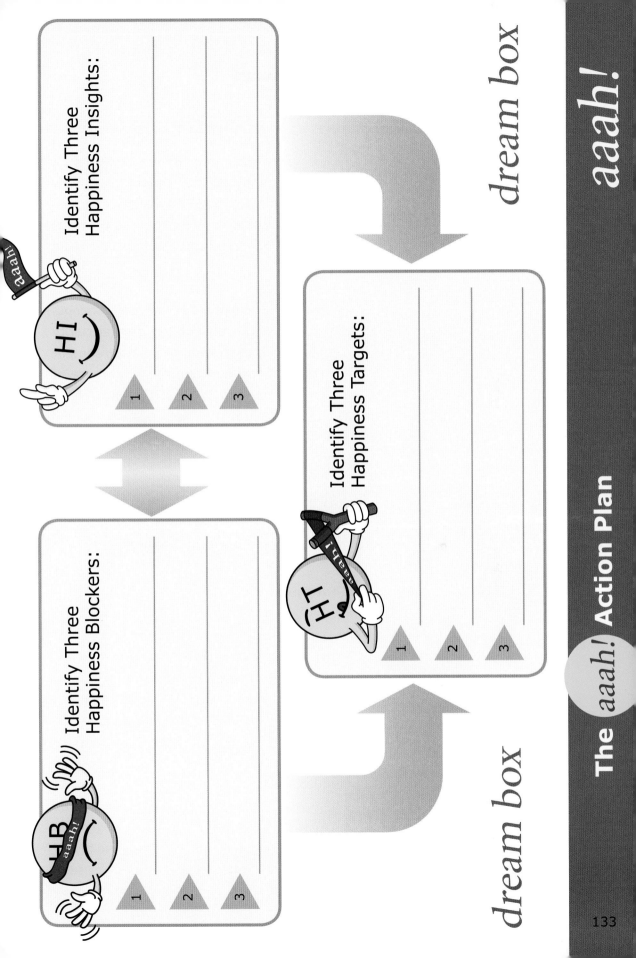

Identify Three
Happiness Insights:

HI

1
2
3

dream box

Identify Three
Happiness Blockers:

HB

1
2
3

dream box

Identify Three
Happiness Targets:

HT

1
2
3

The *aaah!* Action Plan

aaah!

dream box

The Major *Awareness* Takeaways

As you complete the Curious Seeker stage, your activated sense of awareness can be overwhelming—but, try to be grateful! The gift of being awake and present in your life is not something everyone experiences. Many people dismiss personal growth as trivial. They are so boxed in by their ingrained self-limiting beliefs that they have no curiosity to look at their lives and the possibilities that could exist for them in terms of personal growth or new experiences. You are lucky. We will soon see whether you are also a risk taker.

Within the Curious Seeker section, you have experienced several concepts in the aaah! practice model. The exercises have given you greater clarity regarding opportunities for change and growth within your environment and your beliefs as well as in terms of reconnecting to the essence of your original dream for this part of your life. Without this awareness and commitment, you might have drifted in your life because you did not have *fulfillment targets*, so your work here is important. As we close this chapter with some major takeaways, consider the processing and integration you have done throughout this journey so far both in *selfhood* and as we leave the *Curious Seeker* stage.

Major takeaway messages for the Curious Seeker phase are:

aaah! ***Our beliefs drive our behavior***

Whatever you choose to believe, you will behave in accordance with that belief. This directly relates to how you interact with your environment and how you emotionally connect with yourself. To change behavior, you must look to your belief system and become aware of what is driving it. Does this belief empower you or hold you back? What will happen if you abandon this belief? This is why childhood and early adult experiences are so powerful. They shape our belief systems, and we become conditioned to reflect those early beliefs in our adult behaviors. We notice when we hear phrases such as "I was always taught," "When I grew up," or "I was raised to believe." Whether or not they serve us, these are ingrained behaviors and reactions. The question to continuously ask yourself is, is it now time and are you willing to change these beliefs in order to seek the fulfillment you want now in your life?

aaah! An inner voice exists in all of us

From what we do to how we do it, the external world is full of advice. Our inner world and voice are at varying degrees of strength, depending on how much we have nurtured them. We may call these by different names—our inner voice, higher self, or intuition—but each points us to that internal mechanism of being aware of and connected to our sense of self. We need to become more aware of our inner voice, trust its wisdom, and let it guide us toward our dream. The answers are within us, no exceptions.

Depending on your experiences, that inner voice may have been shut down early in life and may have been sent into hiding. I know this was true for me. Unfortunately, many years could go by without this incredible connection to a part of yourself. Increasing your awareness is part of the process of getting it back. You have now initiated this process through the exercises in the Curious Seeker section.

aaah! You have a dream

As a coach, I frequently talk with people about their dreams and aspirations. What I have learned is that there needs to be some time spent reflecting on the essence of the original dream for their lives and what impact that may be having in their lives now. Many people focus only on the role they remember wanting to play as a child and the disappointment they felt if that role was not realized. What is more important now is the essence of the original dream and the potential for embodying that experience now. A child is unlikely to understand the complexity of a dream of being a coach, speaker and an author of a self-help book about personal growth and happiness. Maybe it is just easier to, say, become a doctor, which has the essence of "helping people be better." Remember that there is always enough time in our lives to pursue and realize the experience of our dreams. Always!

I encourage you to continue to reflect on your beliefs, listen to your inner voice, and distill the essence of your original dreams as you continue through this book and further build upon your newfound skills of awareness.

The *aaah!* Practice Model

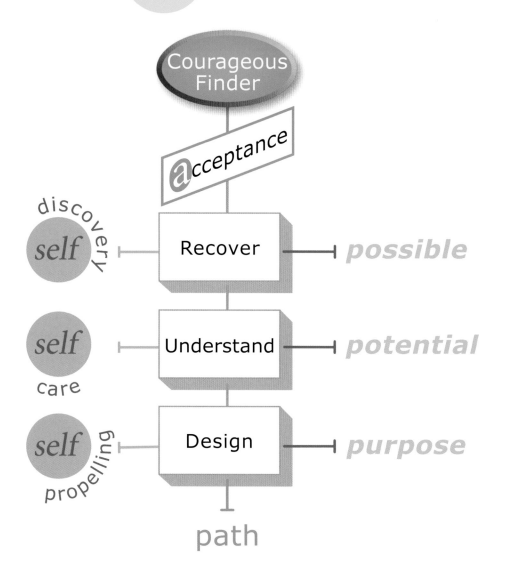

Courageous Finder

acceptance

discovery
self — Recover — *possible*

self — Understand — *potential*
care

self — Design — *purpose*
propelling

path

CHAPTER 9 *aaah!*

The Courageous Finder

Good news! You have cracked open the door to the change and growth process. Awake and alert, the Curious Seeker in you is in the process of mastering the skill of awareness. In addition to surveying your environment, however, you have also initiated a purpose-driven connection between your current beliefs and your original dream. You are clearer about what you want. The question now is whether you are willing to go after it.

In the second phase of the *aaah! practice model*, you are invited to further strengthen your relationship with yourself by doing emotion-based work. Often, self-help books skip this or leave it to the realm of therapists and counselors, but this is the critical link in the change and growth process and what makes the practice of aaah! *a valuable life tool.* Being able to build a relationship with yourself requires you to experience and express your emotions appropriately. You must learn how to open up your heart. When we do this, we can experience rich and fulfilling relationships with ourselves and others—a true happiness experience!

So, will you dismiss this section or choose to engage in it? For some, this is too uncomfortable. If you are practiced at ignoring your feelings and staying completely in your head, this may be especially difficult for you. I know it was initially for me! Remember that you will be able coach yourself through this in the privacy of your own world. **This is a safe place to experiment. I am on your shoulder, ready to help.**

You will be challenged here to confront the issues that you have avoided or ignored in your life because you have not been able to face or resolve them. So, are you ready to walk through the door you have opened and see what is there for you? *Welcome! You are now a Courageous Finder.*

Lean into the Inflection Points

In the Courageous Finder stage, you are encouraged to be personally accountable for your life and to *respond* to your new levels of awareness. You will be asked to take bold and brave actions, both feeling and doing, to move your life forward. This can mean changes in the direction of your career, your environment, or even your relationships. Our routines have the potential to hypnotize us. But now, with our new level of awareness, we can look beyond the trance of the mundane and see what we really want. To get it, we must initiate change. *Yes, initiate it!* We are going to step up to it, grow our way through it, and shape it on purpose.

To make it through this stage, it is best to **lean into the inflection points**. To do so is like riding a bobsled, where you take sharp turns and fast-paced changes in direction by relaxing and leaning into the flow of motion. If you don't, the resistance can cause whiplash. Here, resistance may cause physical and emotional stress that can affect your health. It may also trigger negative self-talk, which may keep you stuck and fearful of change. You will be challenging old beliefs, creating new empowering ones, and changing long-held opinions that are no longer true. Lean into it emotionally and try to minimize the resistance. Be gentle with yourself.

Past emotional experiences often have lingering effects. We are *not concerned with the whys*, but we are interested in **what is here now** so we can ground ourselves and create momentum forward. Events that may have caused us damage are over now. We can carry around the hurt and blame, or we can choose to free ourselves from them.

Remember how our belief system works? Our actions reflect our beliefs. Well, we are going to give that concept a test run here. Of course, to affect this belief system, we will also be directly affecting our behaviors and attitudes. So keep in mind that this process is not going to be a complete secret. The changes we make to our beliefs, while personal and internal, will be visible to our friends and family through our attitudes and behaviors.

Whatever has happened in the past has prepared you to be here now. Whether or not you choose to do the work here, it is work only you can do. Sit and wait? Step up to the challenge?

The Courageous Finder bravely says, "Bring it on!"

We want to come to terms with our emotional issues and have closure. But are we finally ready to release, forgive, let go, or embrace the emotional experiences we have carried with us for much of our lives? It *is time for the Courageous Finder in you to confront reality.* You need to answer these questions honestly, reflecting your personal views rather than the thoughts and expectations of others or even ego-based or saboteur-inspired delusions. As coach, you will need to be on the lookout for this.

Questions the Courageous Finder is dealing with are:

1. Who am I now?

2. Are my current beliefs true for me now?

3. What do I keep, and what do I let go of now?

These questions strike at the core of our being and can be unsettling. Their answers will take our relationships with ourselves to new levels. *The Courageous Finder is ready.*

The Target for the Courageous Finder

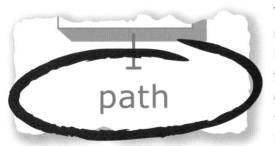

You will recall from the aaah! model that the Courageous Finder is looking for *the path* forward. Having a greater sense of awareness for what he or she wants, the Courageous Finder is ready to create a way to get there. Beyond just observing now, the Courageous Finder must feel his or her way through the process of change and growth and decide what to reclaim and what to claim for the first time, according to his or her *now priorities*.

The path already traveled to get here has been well paved by our experiences. We know every twist and turn; we even collected rocks along the way. Navigating forward from here, however, will require new insights and learning so we can *finally break through and break out* of our self-limiting emotional patterns and stories. The path ahead is unpaved and waiting for its trailblazer. *It's time to make your mark.*

Critical Skill Building: Acceptance

Acceptance is the critical skill for the Courageous Finder. Too often, people mistakenly equate acceptance with surrender. To surrender is to give up and relinquish control or responsibility. Acceptance is quite nearly the opposite. It is about taking ownership for what is ours and releasing from our emotional grasp what is not. We cannot change others. We can, however, change ourselves and, through our responses, influence others. The skill of acceptance is about purposefully choosing a response to secure closure through letting go, embracing, or forgiving. Of course, this process involves others in our lives, but the purpose of doing this is mainly for ourselves. This closure allows us to move forward with our lives**. It is the beginning of your new story**.

Acceptance begins when we take accountability for the experiences in our lives. Parents, partners, bosses, and children are not the ones who determine your experiences—*it is only you.* The implications are straightforward. Are you prepared to roll up your sleeves and clean up any mess or confusion in your life so you can design your path forward and get on your way? It's not easy, but it's worth it!

On my journey, I have spent considerable time in the Courageous Finder stage while attempting to master my personal understanding of acceptance. I just could not get over how everything could have been different, **"if only."** I was angry and frustrated and wanted to explode when I replayed the tapes of my life experiences in my mind. I could go on for days (and did for years). My partner deserves an award for listening to my ongoing drama so lovingly. I was convinced I was misunderstood and underestimated. And you know what? It was true.

The hardest part to accept was that I was the one misunderstanding and underestimating myself. After much denial, over time, and with a struggle, I was finally ready to take responsibility for who I was, where I was, and what I had done to create this experience. Most important, I was ready to accept my *selfhood* and see my path forward, whereas before, I could see only the wall. The wall was the mental image of people and things that were between my desires and their realization. After a while, that wall changed to a fence. I had believed the fence was locking me into my circumstances, and I finally came to understand that it was not—it had always been unlocked. I just had to go over and let myself out. I had the power the whole time, just like Dorothy in *The Wizard of Oz*. This realization that the power of choice is always within us is the ultimate demonstration of mastering the skill of acceptance.

Our ability to use our acceptance skills has important outcomes:

1. *We get real with ourselves*, and we let go, forgive, and bring closure to the emotional turmoil with which we have struggled. In cleaning out our emotional closets, we open our hearts further. This creates space and time we can now apply toward *growing forward.*

2. *It forces us to face our illusions* regarding what could be if we wait long enough for others to change. We can change only ourselves.

Get Real with Yourself

Before racing toward our new path, we need to accept our current reality. *We need to clean up, clean out, and resolve the issues that have restrained us so we can make a fresh start*. Are you feeling trapped by obligations and commitments to others? Have you lost the time, energy, and self-confidence to pursue your desires? We are now going to explore the **Recover, Understand,** and **Design** boxes on the model. Now you will be asked to take a position for yourself and ensure that your needs are prioritized first. You can give back once you have something to give. Get out your diagnostic again. *Let's focus on your path forward.*

aaah-*cceptance* Coaching Tip

Let's try some exercises to build our acceptance skills. This will help you choose appropriate responses in emotional situations.

1. Set an intention to be emotionally present and accept whatever appears in your life today. Promise yourself that you will let go of something with which you normally would take issue. Be prepared to smile, take a deep breath, and embrace any situation you are presented with that causes disruption to your day. In setting these intentions, you proactively create space between you and your instinctual emotional reactions. You are accepting responsibility for your emotional responses. Make a brief journal entry on your experience.

2. Catch yourself in the act of negative self-talk. Decide that when you notice it, you will respond to negative self-talk by stopping immediately and spending the subsequent three to five minutes talking to yourself positively. Tell yourself how wonderful you are, what you are proud of in your life, or how appreciative you are to have these few minutes for nurturing yourself. You are accepting accountability for your thoughts and are positively putting them to work for you.

Developing the skill of acceptance will take practice. Empowered with it, we can choose to have closure with our emotions and manage emotionally charged situations more comfortably. *Acceptance* is, in fact, our critical second skill in our pursuit of change, growth, and happiness. It is the second powerful piece of the *aaah!* acronym.

The Recover Box

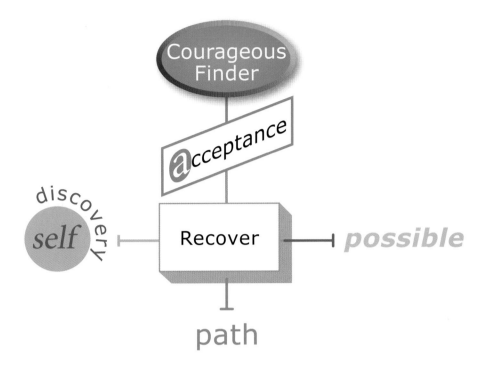

The **Recover box** is first in the Courageous Finder stage. Here, you will be taking back pieces of you that were lost or given away and that you now need for your selfhood journey to continue forward. This could be extra time given to work, self-esteem lost to a bad relationship, or perhaps time alone given up for childcare or eldercare responsibilities. Again, you will be asked to consider the perspective of *self-discovery* to see what is possible, but this time you are not an observer of the environment; you are an active participant. The challenge in this context is to change the direction and the dynamic of how you are interacting *within* your environment. You must change your energy flow from giving to taking. *You will also need to set up new boundaries to maintain your sense of self once it is recovered.*

Your Personal Declaration Statement

An exercise I created while struggling through my Courageous Finder stage was developing a personal declaration statement, a list of 10 to 15 promises I made to myself in the areas of physical health, emotional balance and behavior, intellectual pursuits, and spiritual activities.

In creating yours, select a cross section of promises that represent what you are working on in your life. When you read it, your reaction should be: ***Yes! This is what I want to feel, believe, and experience!*** If the statements on the page don't resonate with you like this, change them. Type it out, use colors to highlight your most descriptive words, print it, and make copies and place them where they are in your view every day. I have one on my bathroom mirror, one in the front pocket of my journal, and one under a paperweight on my desk. Keep your intentions, commitments, and promises visible to you and they will materialize more quickly.

Stay Focused on the Path

Change and growth require focus, discipline, and persistence. We have to manage ourselves, but we also have friends and family who have vested interests and who, through their interactions with us, may try to keep us stuck because it is comfortable and familiar to them. *The entire system wants to maintain the status quo.* To pursue our new or modified path, we must coach ourselves into staying the course. Our path will be a winding road with hills and valleys. We will want to stop. This is a natural response to the challenge of change. Our motivation for continuing forward is getting to experience the happiness we have targeted for ourselves. Actually, we can already start to enjoy this happiness while traveling the road because the journey is the experience. When we are on our right path, we will feel the fit and comfort immediately. *Work out the path.*

The work of the Courageous Finder involves emotional processing time. Identify a peaceful surrounding where you can relax and immerse yourself in this exploration.

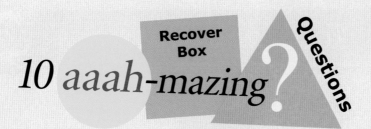

Recover Box

10 aaah-mazing **Questions**

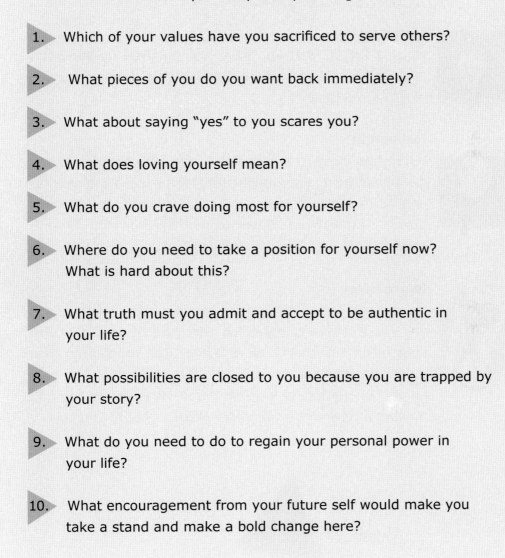

Remember to stay focused on the area of your life
for which you completed your diagnostic.

1. Which of your values have you sacrificed to serve others?

2. What pieces of you do you want back immediately?

3. What about saying "yes" to you scares you?

4. What does loving yourself mean?

5. What do you crave doing most for yourself?

6. Where do you need to take a position for yourself now?
   What is hard about this?

7. What truth must you admit and accept to be authentic in
   your life?

8. What possibilities are closed to you because you are trapped by
   your story?

9. What do you need to do to regain your personal power in
   your life?

10. What encouragement from your future self would make you
    take a stand and make a bold change here?

These questions provide opportunities for reflection. You may choose
to ponder them or actively experience them through journaling,
meditating, or creating a visualization board to provide you with an
enriched context for creating your change momentum.

Tools and Treasures

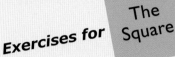

Exercises for The Square

Illumination
Make a list of what you have lost or given up and want back in this part of your life. Note specifically what it is and where it went.

Reflection
What has been the emotional cost (frustration, anger, disappointment, depression) for not taking ownership for your own best interests (lost opportunities for personal growth, professional development, relationships)? Write briefly about your feelings and desires.

Expression
In your self-talk, both positive and negative, what feelings are you expressing regarding this part of your life? Are your feelings authentic or reflexive? Call yourself on this. Challenge whether you are mindful or mindless in your emotional chatter. Is it keeping you stuck or moving you forward in rewriting your story? Make a note to yourself.

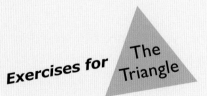

Exercises for The Triangle

Illumination
Make a list of what you want to stop, start, and continue accepting in this area of your life.

Reflection

List recent compromises you made where the needs of others were placed above your own. For each compromise, write short notes for what you will do next time to ensure that your needs are met first.

Expression

List 10 affirmations that express positive feelings you would like to embrace in your life. Make copies. Place them where you will notice them: in your car, in your briefcase, inside the cover of a book, in your bathroom magazine rack. Promise to read them several times a day.

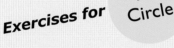

Exercises for The Circle

Illumination

Looking ahead at the next year, what emotional challenge do you need to accept now to ensure that you continue to move forward and grow on your path? Write it here.

Reflection

You are sharing a story about yourself with a child. What lessons and experiences have emotionally shaped you into being the type of person you are today in this part of your life? What examples would you give? Write them here.

Expression

What advice would you offer newlyweds about managing their individual needs and boundaries as they enter their new partnership together? Write a few words.

recover box

A Plan of Action for the Recover Box

Having completed the exercises in your shape score or perhaps even venturing beyond and doing more, you have had a chance to expand your thinking about this area of your life. Hopefully, you gained some new perspectives and were stimulated to have creatively explored different ways to consider your challenges and opportunities.

We will now specifically take this learning and turn it into actions that can move you forward. *Here again is where the coach within steps up!*

Take a few minutes to review your answers to the aaah-mazing questions and your responses to the experiential exercises. Consider thoughtfully, with an open heart, what you need to address and deal with here. What is draining you or holding you back from having all that you need within you to experience your happiness?

You will now be given a chance to map out an action plan for you to shape this part of your life in a new way. Here is how it works:

Happiness Blockers (HB)

Identify the three major obstacles (physical or emotional) you have in this particular area of your life. Write them in the spaces on the action plan page.

Happiness Insights (HI)

On the basis of your answers from the questions, the experiential exercises, and your internal vision for what the path to happiness looks like for you in this part of your life, identify three new pieces of learning or insights about your environment or current circumstances that you did not see or consider in this way before. Write them in the spaces on the action plan page.

Happiness Target (HT)

Now define three actions (they can be doing or feeling) you can take that will be a commitment to you moving toward creating your path forward in this area of your life. Make them things you can, in fact, control and accomplish. Make them exciting enough to strive for!

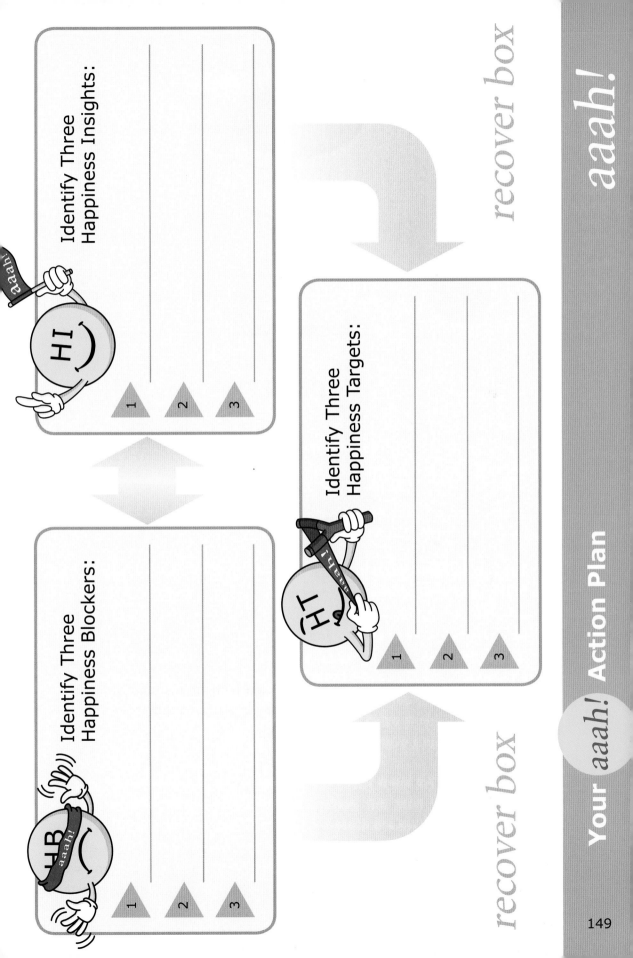

Identify Three Happiness Insights:

1
2
3

Identify Three Happiness Blockers:

1
2
3

Identify Three Happiness Targets:

1
2
3

recover box

recover box

Your *aaah!* Action Plan

149

The Understand Box

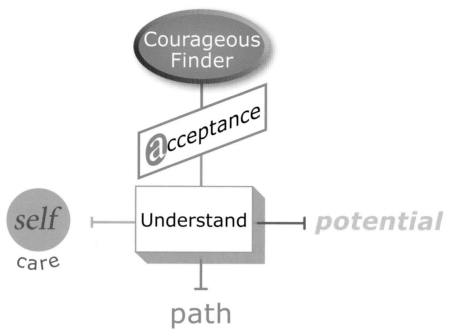

Courageous Finder

acceptance

self care — Understand — *potential*

path

Here you need to ask yourself whether you are facilitating or blocking your change process. You may be causing active or passive interference because you are emotionally attached to your story or a perspective that is not true, does not serve you, or does not matter. So you may not get traction on your path because you are holding back your personal potential. In my own journey, I found this box to be the hardest one.

The Understanding box is where we finally confront the collection of old hurts, disappointments, and memories we have experienced and that we continue to carry around with us like a backpack full of rocks. We are so affected by these events and experiences that we are unable to let go and move on. Instead we have *memorialized and immortalized* them and have chosen to collect them. We can say, "Look at this rock: this is when my mother did this to me," and "Yeah, if you think that stinks, look at this rock: this is when my boss did that." With these rocks, we repeat these stories and events over and over again.

Intellectually, we know these rocks weigh us down and serve no positive purpose. They limit our potential energy and momentum for moving forward; maybe we are scared of our own potential for success. Holding onto this backpack of rocks somehow excuses us from being able to move briskly along our path—so you can't really fail because you were handicapped with the rocks to begin with. Maybe you just believe that some people are meant to carry these backpack burdens.

Either way, the Understanding box is an opportunity to clean out the emotional weights you have been carrying around and lighten your load. This makes room for the sweeping positive energy of change to flow through you.

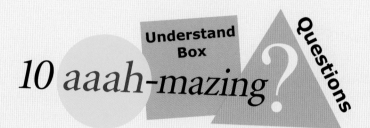

10 aaah-mazing?
Understand Box
Questions

1. What does it feel like to trust that things will unfold exactly as they should?

2. What does letting go and forgiving feel like in this part of your life?

3. If everything you've experienced in your life, good and bad, was designed to bring you to this exact place, what would letting go from this perspective look like? How would it be easier or more difficult?

4. What does it feel like to be told you are a magnificent person with amazing talents and gifts?

5. What is the impact of letting go of the guilt and disappointment you hold onto in this area of your life?

6. What does forgiving those who have hurt you feel like?

7. How would your view of yourself be changed by believing that everyone had both shadow and light parts to their personalities and that we needed to express both to be whole in our lives?

8. What is hard about opening your heart (further)?

9. If the strength of a relationship is determined by how quickly you forgive and move forward after an emotional outburst, how strong are your relationships with others? With yourself?

10. What could you say to those you have hurt that would allow you to forgive and embrace yourself in this part of your life?

Tools and Treasures

Exercises for The Square

Illumination

Write five to 10 negative thoughts you say to yourself regarding this part of your life. Be honest. Get a tape recorder. Read your complete list slowly and clearly five times, continuously. Listen to the tape. Rewind and listen again. How does it feel? What was the experience like to hear this abuse over and over? Write your feelings.

Reflection

Write 10 regrets in this part of your life. At the bottom of the page, write that you are sorry, you forgive yourself, and you are now willing to let go. Sign it. Date it. Choose to throw it away, shred it, or burn it. This physical action can stimulate an emotional response. Write your feelings about this experience.

Expression

Make a list of the people you need emotional closure with in this part of your life. Get a stack of index cards. Write a short note to each that expresses this closure. Sign it and date it. Now choose to either destroy the notes or communicate them if appropriate. Write your feelings about the experience.

Exercises for The Triangle

Illumination

Remember that voice that plays in our heads? We may call it our gremlin, ego, or saboteur. Notice the one that pops up for you in this area of your life. Give it a name. Now have a conversation with that character in your mind. Tell it that you understand its concern and appreciate the help. Explain that you are fine and have the situation under control. Now, create a gesture to pat it on the head or give it a hug to calm it down. Thank it and send it away. Take yourself through this process whenever you feel it popping up. With the voice out of your way, your true self can more accurately and appropriately deal with the problem or situation in front of you. Write the name you chose for this gremlin/saboteur so you can refer to it when necessary.

Reflection

Get ready to clean out your emotional closets and throw away the baggage taking up room in your heart and mind. Find the music you listen to when you want to go back and experience those hurts and disappointments. You know where it is! Play each song. After each song, write on an index card one to two sentences that give you closure with this experience. Create a ceremony for destroying the cards and therefore metaphorically release them from your heart and mind. It may take some time, but a day or so invested here can free your world. Get listening. When you have completed this activity, make a journal entry about the experience. What was the process like as you went through it? How do you feel having completed it?

Expression

Physical activity is a great way to process and release what is locked up inside of you. Enroll in a yoga class, get on the stationary bike, take a hike, or walk and breathe deeply. A regular practice of exercise will get the stagnant energy out of you and will make room for fresh new energy. This is not an overnight or one-time activity, but with time, you will have processed your pain and developed better fitness. Go move your body.

Exercises for The Circle

Illumination

List seven to 10 wonderful things you say to yourself when you engage in positive self-talk. Get a tape recorder out and read the complete list slowly and clearly, five consecutive times, into the recorder. Rewind and listen. Make a few notes about how it feels to listen to this over and over again.

Reflection

When you were growing up, what inspiration or encouragement did you receive from your parents, grandparents, or other adults? What influence did this have on who you are today in this area of your life? Write these people thank-you notes for giving you this gift of encouragement and support. Choose to send them or save them for yourself.

Expression

Use your intuition to select two members from your advisory board. Sit quietly and ask them what message they have for you in this part of your life. Write the messages.

understand box

A Plan of Action for the Understand Box

It's time for action again. *Please refer to the Recover box action plan for more detailed instructions on how to proceed.*

On the basis of your answers to the aaah-mazing questions and your responses to the experiential exercises, you are going to develop an action plan for forward movement in creating your path.

Happiness Blockers (HB)

Identify the three major obstacles (physical or emotional) you have in this particular area of your life. Write them in the spaces on the action plan page.

Happiness Insights (HI)

Using your answers from the aaah-mazing questions, the experiential exercises, and your own happiness goals, identify three happiness insights that demonstrate your optimism about your potential for creating your path forward in this area of your life. Write them in the spaces on the action plan page.

Happiness Target (HT)

Now define three actions (doing or feeling) you can take that will be a commitment to moving forward on your path in this area of your life. Make them things you can, in fact, control and accomplish. Make them exciting enough to strive for!

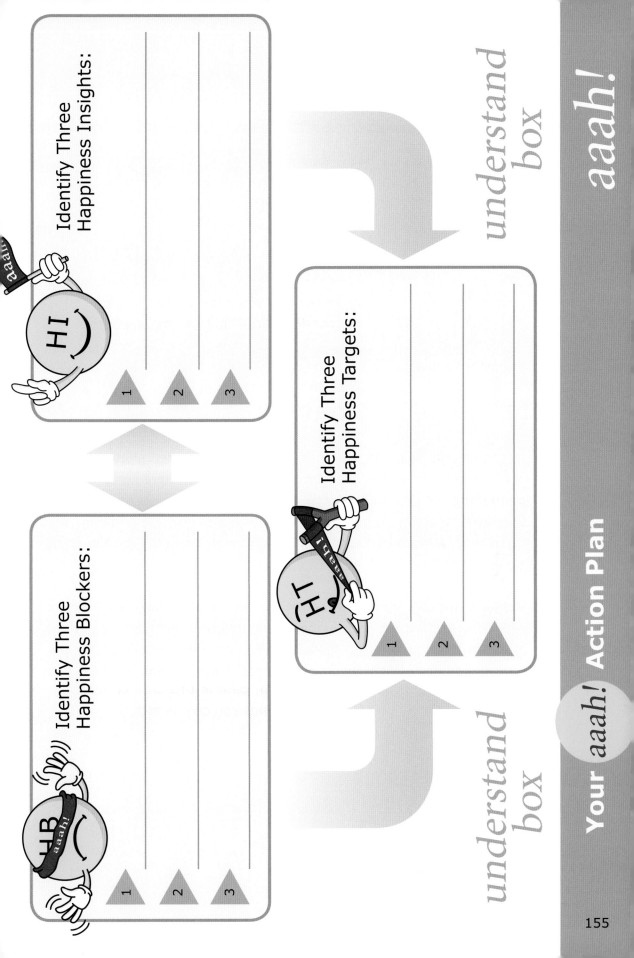

Identify Three
Happiness Insights:

1

2

3

Identify Three
Happiness Blockers:

1

2

3

Identify Three
Happiness Targets:

1

2

3

understand box

understand box

Your *aaah!* Action Plan

aaah!

155

The Design Box

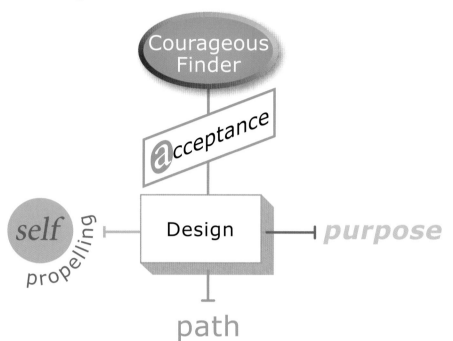

In the Design box, the last in the Courageous Finder phase, we are again *leaning into the inflection point* of change. Here we are **self-propelling** forward with energy and momentum toward our purpose. We have the ability to be the architect of the life we are creating, and our blueprint, or, in this case, our design, helps us to lay out the steps we need to take.

We want to experience our dreams. We also want to make a difference with our lives, but we are weighed down by questions. Can we get out of our own way and make this happen? Is it too late? Do we have the time and energy? Of course, the answer is that it is never too late; just choose and take action. **You can get there from here!**

10 aaah-mazing Questions

Design Box

Remember to stay focused on the area of your life
for which you completed your diagnostic.

1. What feelings do you associate with having a plan for
   your path?

2. What is the plan you have right now for your path forward?

3. How do you feel about getting started on your path?

4. What choices you are considering for your path forward?
   What is the energy of each?

5. How do you feel about your ability to select a direction for
   your path?

6. What is holding you back right now?

7. What is waiting for you on the path once you choose it?

8. In taking this path, what would you be leaving behind?

9. What is the next step you can take now regarding your path?

10. What declaration can you make out loud that confirms
    your intention to move forward toward your purpose?

Tools and Treasures

Exercises for **The Square**

Illumination

Write the various choices and considerations you currently have for your path forward in this part of your life. If there are a few that naturally belong in the same group or theme, put them together. For each theme, select one word that describes the essence of the choices. Do you see any patterns emerging? Make a priority list for yourself based on your excitement level for the preferences. Make a few notes for yourself.

Reflection

Imagine a time when you were experiencing peak performance. You may have been speaking to a group, playing a sport, or telling a great story. What were you doing? What were the reactions of others who were witnessing you? What type of feedback did you receive? How did it make you feel? What about that experience do you want to bring forward as you determine your path in this part of your life? Capture a few notes on this.

Expression

Imagine you are a human piece of metal. A huge magnet is pulling and attracting you toward it. The power and force are so strong you cannot resist. What are you being pulled toward in this area of your life? Say it out loud. What steps do you need to take to move you toward that attractive place? Write a few notes to yourself.

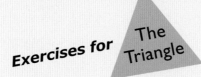

Exercises for **The Triangle**

Illumination

As you consider the paths available to you in this part of your life, assessing their strengths and weaknesses may be helpful. Make two columns on a page, and on the left side, list your top two preferred paths. On the right side, list another two that you are considering in your due diligence but that you have less heart for. Consider the opportunities and limitations for each choice. Do any new choices

158

or combinations emerge? Consider passing these ideas by your advisory team for insights and perspective. Now make a choice, for right now, on one of the options that feels exciting. Make a few short notes and map out the first two or three steps for a plan on how to move forward. Decide to go out and experience this choice. You can always choose again.

Reflection

For the path you are about to take, what type of shoes do you need? Describe them (sneakers for speed, sturdy boots for climbing) and the supplemental supplies you wish to have handy on your journey. You are metaphorically packing for an important trip, so be prepared. Write what you need.

Expression

What intentions regarding your path would you declare to the universe if you knew absolutely that they would come true and you could not fail? Write them here.

Exercises for **The Circle**

Illumination:

Draw three concentric circles on a piece of paper. Your life is now the center circle. Your desire is to share more of your learning and insights with others. How can you extend your wisdom? Make a few notes on what each expansive circle means as a next step for you in this area of your life.

Reflection

Look at yourself in a mirror. Give yourself a minute to take in all that you are, all that you've done, and all that you still have to do. Acknowledge yourself for the amazing person you are. Commit to yourself that you will fulfill your destiny and walk your path as a gift to yourself and to the world. Write a few sentences about what this experience feels like.

Expression

You are speaking to a group of people who are at a crossroads in their lives and who are trying to choose a path forward. What advice can you offer them about your journey and decision-making process? How can you inspire them to accept accountability for their lives and their choices? How might you inspire their courage? Write the wisdom or advice you would share.

A Plan of Action for the Design Box

Please refer to the Recover box action plan for more detailed instructions on how to proceed.

On the basis of your answers to the aaah-mazing questions and your responses to the experiential exercises, develop your action plan for forward movement.

Happiness Blockers (HB)

Identify the three major obstacles (physical or emotional) you have in this particular area of your life. Write them in the spaces on the action plan page.

Happiness Insights (HI)

On the basis of your answers from the questions, the experiential exercises, and your own goals, identify three happiness insights that demonstrate your optimism about what is possible for you energetically as you move toward your purpose. Write them in the spaces on the action plan page.

Happiness Target (HT)

Now define three actions (doing or feeling) you can take that will be a commitment to you moving toward your purpose and on your path heading for what you want in this area of your life. Make them things you can control and accomplish. Make them exciting enough to strive for!

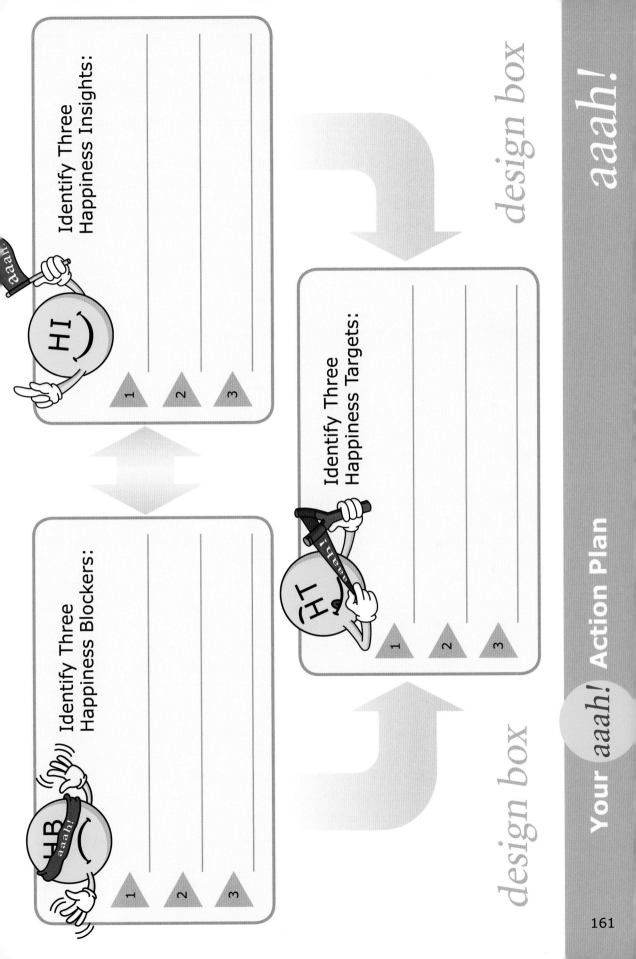

Identify Three
Happiness Insights:

HI

1
2
3

Identify Three
Happiness Blockers:

HB

1
2
3

Identify Three
Happiness Targets:

HT

1
2
3

design box

design box

Your *aaah!* Action Plan

aaah!

161

The Major *Acceptance* Takeaways

In the Courageous Finder stage, you were called into the reality of taking accountability for your life. Here you began to take positions on behalf of yourself, cleaned out your emotional closet, and started to get rid of the accumulated baggage. This was a process of emotionally recalibrating yourself into balance so that you could turn your energy toward creating the experiences you want to have.

Major takeaway messages for the Courageous Finder phase are:

aaah!   ***You are a mixture of influences***

Throughout childhood and early adulthood, you have been heavily influenced by external factors. You have had rules to follow, expectations to live up to, and roles to play. If you were lucky, your talents emerged and were nurtured and encouraged enough to develop into your unique gifts in this lifetime.

Sometimes, unfortunately, our talents are hard to see initially, are totally missed, or are basically disregarded. The inner voice expression of our wants and desires may not have had the chance to get noticed and, without focus and development, may have gotten entirely lost. In these cases, external influences will have dominated our lives. So, we develop skills for competently performing in jobs or roles that are socially relevant but for which we have no passion—that is, until we get to *selfhood.* Here, we recalibrate and reconsider the changes we want or need to make. We need to recover the strength of that inner voice that had a plan for us and work with it to shape what is next.

The mixture of influences needs to be sorted through now so you can keep what you need and let go of what you don't. This could be releasing beliefs that no longer work for you or taking back time and energy you gave away to others while sacrificing your own needs. You need to recover your balance and become your whole self again. As a child, you were told when to get away from people and things that were bad influences. *Well, this is the selfhood version.*

aaah! *Nurture and self-parent your way through*

Courageous Finders learn to accept that they have everything they need. Within us is the power to heal, accept, forgive, let go, embrace, and anything else we need. Accepting this insight is critical to building our relationship with ourselves because it solidifies selfhood through self-reliance and self-sufficiency. *You don't need to prove yourself to others; only your expectations need to be met.* We no longer have to give endlessly to others with the hope of maybe receiving at some point. We can choose to generously give to ourselves. Remember the last time you were on an airplane and heard the instructions to put the oxygen mask on yourself first? This is the same principle. You must ensure your own well-being in order to be able to survive, thrive, and ultimately give back to others.

You have had a chance here to sort through baggage, remind yourself of what you love, and toss out what is too small, too tight, and just not your style anymore.

aaah! *Make your dreams come true*

We learned from the Curious Seeker phase that reconnecting with our original dream and **distilling its essence** are wonderful possibilities for us to pursue at any time. We may have even been lulled into fantasizing about how great life will be when we arrive in *dreamland.*

Welcome to dream boot camp. The Courageous Finder stage is where you dropped the fantasy and started creating the plan and walking the path. **Enough wishing and hoping—it's time for shaping and doing.** To take our dreams from abstract to actualized experiences, we needed to design a path. The *what* was established in our Curious Seeker phase, and the possible *which ways* we explored as the Courageous Finder. *Remember to stay flexible*. If you are looking for freedom and abundance, for example, these may show up in the form of money, homes, and vacations, or, alternatively, you could be the recipient of more time, space, and comfort. Set your sight on the path and see how the possibilities unfold for you.

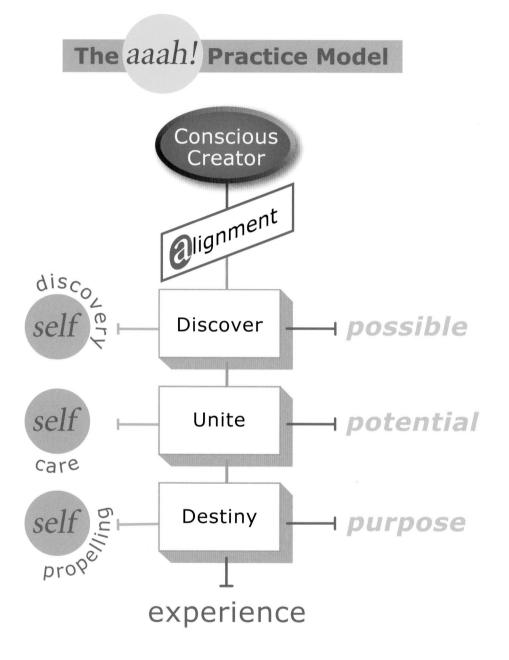

The Conscious Creator

Welcome forward! It's time to bring together the insights you've gained and the hard work you've done so that tangible experiential outcomes result. Your possible choices will become clear here: the potential in you fully emerges, and where you need to be to have the experience you want is right where you are standing—that is, of course, if you continue with your *selfhood* process and remain willing to shape your life on purpose.

Remember that before becoming a Curious Seeker, you were unconsciously aware of who you were and what you wanted. You were going through the motions of acting out your life. The script was handed to you, and you dutifully read it. You then began to sense your own internal desire for something more, to express yourself from your heart, and to speak your truth. But to do this, you needed to write yourself out of the old script or story of your life and start developing a new one. You started to become more conscious about your life and how it was unfolding. You even identified or remembered the dream role you always wanted to play.

As a Courageous Finder, you have come to terms with aspects of your life that were not working optimally for you. You mustered up the internal fortitude to break free and finally go out on your own. You assumed authorship for your life and began to script your own lines and new stories. *You found your authentic voice within yourself.* So, here you are now, ready to take these newfound skills and apply them to creating your life in your way. The greatest story ever imagined and lived is about to unfold for you. You want to integrate what you now know and authentically experience your life here in this and every moment. You are a Conscious Creator!

Resolve the Tensions

To harness the transformative energy we need to **self-propel** ourselves forward in this final stage of the growth and change process, we need to *resolve the tensions* that we have created, in part, through our work on this journey. In doing this, we fortify and strengthen the internal energy we are building. Remember that change is a dynamic system, so any adjustments we make in one place will have resultant effects in another place.

Within ourselves, we have created tension between our active conscious state and our unconscious passive state of existence. Staying present and mindful takes effort and practice. It also gets easier with time. Resolving tension here is the result of increasing our time consciously spent in an active, mindful state and resisting the temptations to slip back into a passive role in our life. This concentration and focus will, in part, be fueled by what we now learn here as a Conscious Creator.

Our progression through the various phases of the aaah! model inevitably creates new wants, needs, and beliefs. This causes a different kind of tension to develop inside ourselves, almost like a internal tug-of-war. We are fixated on developing and projecting our new and emerging selves while at the same time we are frustrated by our continuing breakthrough experiences of our old selves showing up. So we shift between wanting to completely adopt our new persona and yet at times being pulled into our old habits because they are comfortable and familiar. This internal tension is an important lesson for us. As we stop to examine it more closely for a moment, we notice that *this tension is actually working to pull these selves together into cohesion* rather than pushing each away and creating resistance. It is like a compelling magnetic force attracting and integrating what belongs together.

As we resolve this tension within ourselves, it is important to note that our relationships with others will also be affected. Again, *remember that we are working with a system*. As friends and family feel and notice the changes in us, their reactions might be to unconsciously or consciously create resistance. This will be experienced as strain and tension in these relationships. We will need to resolve these tensions as a Courageous Finder, of course, by reworking our way through the Recover and Understanding boxes for this relationship—*an example of how we are present in all three stages of the model simultaneously as we work on our personal growth.*

Like many things in life, resolving tension is a continuous process. It requires that we develop new beliefs and ensure that they are ingrained. But even with them firmly in place, as we continue to learn, tension will arise as we are challenged by new thoughts or new views on old thoughts. Remember our **circulinear** learning process? This is also an important concept in the Conscious Creator stage. As we complete our work in one area of our lives, we are completing a loop on the circulinear learning process. Still, life and learning continue, and we can already feel that as we finish our work in this section and enter a new place, we will have a calling to the next place on our journey. Think of resolving the tension in part as having closure, like hitting a pause button to process life for a short period and then choosing to start again!

Only when we are able to resolve these various tensions can we fully embody the role of the Conscious Creator. We need to unite our internal energy and then align it with our desires so we can finally be in *a state of aaah*! It is in bringing together what we want and how we feel and through giving voice to our intentions that we create and subsequently have the opportunity to *allow ourselves to have the experience*! In these moments, we are integrated, whole, authentic, and living our lives on purpose. We experience peace within ourselves, and we are fulfilled and happy!

Aligning Our Shadow and Light

We have different parts to our personalities; we love some and loathe others. They are sometimes referred to as our shadow and light. The darker parts of our personalities exist in the shadows. These may include our bad temper, stubborn streak, or jealous tendencies. We try not to allow them to be in plain view of everyone, as they may reflect poorly on the person we wish to be. The lighter parts of our personality are what we most often show the outside world, which could be our humor, warmth, honesty, and charm. *However, both the light and the dark sides of us have roles to play in bringing our authentic selves forward.* When we resolve this tension within us and allow all parts of ourselves to be accepted, appreciated, and expressed as part of our integrated whole being, this allows us to be our authentic selves. No more secrets. No more hiding. We are free to use our true voices in the world in the pursuit of our happiness and well-being. When we achieve this, we reach a state of ease and comfort with ourselves—*a feeling that we are comfortable in our own skin.*

In the Courageous Finder stage, we spent some time in the Understanding box and worked on examining these concepts. You may remember that we forgave ourselves and embraced as well as let go of some of the experiences we had from indulging in the shadow parts of our personalities. *Our shadow sides have lessons to teach us as well, and we need to embrace them as parts of ourselves.* Through our awareness and acceptance, we give our shadow and the undesirable personality traits less power as we allow our light to become dominant. Getting our energy balance right allows us to put our best self forward and to put our intentions to more productive use!

The Conscious Creator is, first and foremost, *a constant decision maker.* We have full control and flexibility if we choose to use it. Once we make a choice, we must align ourselves to feel and believe that it is what we want. ***Giving our choices both thought based and emotional focus creates the energy we need for them to materialize as experiences.*** Once we have the experience, we either choose to continue or select again. *This is shaping life on purpose and creating happiness.*

The questions that guide us as a Conscious Creator are:

1. What choices do I make now?

2. Do these choices support my best interests?

3. Am I being who I am meant to be in my life?

In these questions, we challenge ourselves to confirm that we are making our choices in accordance with our values and our authentic selves. If we do, we ensure that we are choosing the life we are meant to be living. These are exciting and inspiring checkpoints for daily life.

The Target for the Conscious Creator

You will recall from the aaah! model that the Conscious Creator is looking for ***the experience.*** He or she knows that life is lived here, now, and in the moment. *Possessions and destinations are only distractions from what really matters.*

Conscious Creators master how to experience their lives on their terms. They have already confirmed the ***what*** and the ***where***; now they select among the choices for the ***which*** one and quickly evaluate whether this is the experience they want. If not, they need only select again and see whether an alternative selection is better. Confident in their instincts, they move through their lives and know that they will arrive at the experiences that deeply connect who they are with what they should be doing.

Critical Skill Building: Alignment

We all know what it feels like when everything seems to just fall into place and work out perfectly. When it does happen, we relish it. Wouldn't it be great to have these types of experiences more often? What if we could influence or even create these circumstances so that the proverbial sun, moon, and stars could be lined up at our request?

Bringing yourself into alignment unlocks a power that compels the tools and opportunities that you need to achieve for your happiness target to fall into place. You may have heard about the Law of Attraction—the belief that when you state a wish or intention, the universe immediately goes to work to bring it to you. This is a concept that has been highly publicized and yet often misinterpreted. *It is not magic—but it is also not as simple as merely making a wish.* It is purposeful thought, feeling, and voiced intention being directed to your desire. As you know from the chapter on the connections of change, growth, and happiness, once you have laid the foundation for a new belief, you will seek and find those experiences that confirm it. This is the essence of the Law of Attraction put into the fundamental change process language. However, there are no simple buttons to press for easy answers. **Changing your life takes purpose and practice.**

To use the skill of alignment, the Conscious Creator must have had what I call a *precipitating event*. He or she has made a decision or choice about what to bring to fruition by way of an experience. To realize the full experience, the Conscious Creator must also be completely vested in the choice—no doubts, no second-guessing. It's like being at the amusement park: you have to choose the next ride. If you choose to ride the Ferris wheel and all the while wonder what it would be like if you were on the roller coaster, you miss the entire experience. Enjoy the ride you're on. You can always choose another one later!

This is where many people have trouble. They are unwilling to choose and end up spending their time in indecision instead of action. *Making a choice feels, to some, like scarcity or limitation. In reality, choice pursued with conviction creates abundance because you have the whole entire experience.* Without definitive and conscious choice, you really experience nothing! Without choice, you are simply living in a world of contemplation, lost in your own mind of possibilities, never benefiting from the feeling of the experience, which is what you are after.

In my own journey, I have noticed that when what I want is not happening or moving forward, it is my own lack of clarity in choosing that is the obstacle. Once I do clearly make my choice and I confidently align myself with it, everything starts to unfold quickly. It sounds simple, but to practice it consistently and intentionly can be challenging.

Our ability to use our alignment skills has important outcomes:

1. It is an *integrated skill* that requires that our mind, heart, and voice be in the same place as our choices. The presence of all of these pieces will result in bringing our desires to fruition. If we are not using the power of all of these elements, we are less likely to create our intention. *So simultaneous thinking, feeling, and being able to voice a clear intention are critical to the skill of alignment.*

2. It has an effect of *creating illumination* in our lives. We are no longer anticipating what we want our experience to be; we are having it! In the experience, we can know whether our choice was good. We can process real learning, and then we have the opportunity to make another better-informed decision based on that experience—true illumination.

Get out There!

As a Curious Seeker, your challenge was to **get clear** on what you wanted. The Courageous Finder in you needed to see reality and **get real** with yourself. The Conscious Creator needs to **get out there** in the world and live the experience you desire. Move yourself beyond the possible choices to make a selection and create the experience. We will explore some of these areas more deeply as we now make our way through the **Discover, Unite,** and **Destiny** boxes in the model.

The Discover Box

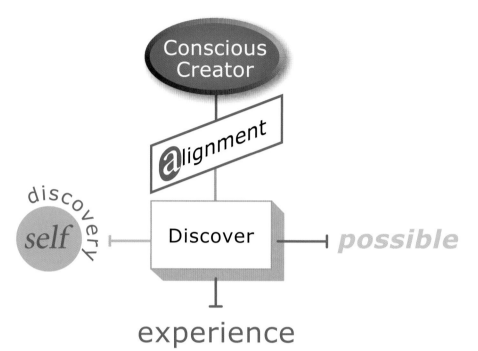

The Discover box is first in the Conscious Creator section, and it looks at our range of choices and possibilities for *now creating what we want in our environment*. Our challenge is to resist the temptation of continuously evaluating and considering the options available and to make a choice—any choice, really. If we don't like the experience from this one, we can choose another. We have done the hard work before we got here, so we know what we are after. *Now only through choice can we create the experience and see whether it fulfills our desire*. The critical piece is that we select from the possibilities and choose an experience.

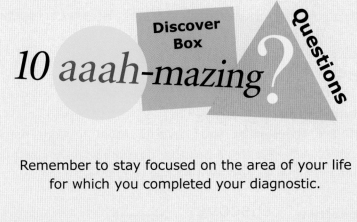

Discover Box

10 *aaah-mazing* ?

Questions

Remember to stay focused on the area of your life
for which you completed your diagnostic.

1. What choices are possible in this environment right now?

2. What is one possible expression for your vision of your future
    right now?

3. What, if anything, is keeping you from choosing and creating the
    experience you want?

4. What personal growth opportunity can you take advantage of in
    this environment?

5. What are you learning about yourself as a decision maker?

6. What is your process for narrowing the possible choices here?

7. What is the hardest part for you in making a choice?

8. How does it feel to stand on the edge of choosing what you want
    to create in this area of your life?

9. What is hard for you to express about what you want here?

10. What do you need to see or know that would make you confident
    in expressing what you want?

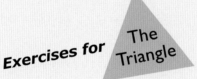

Exercises for The Square

Illumination

You are redesigning your favorite room in your home. Your architect asks for three possible directions to play with. How do you direct him or her? Write a few thoughts.

Reflection

You are planning a vacation of a lifetime. Your three favorite destinations all have great packages and great weather, and all the dates work for you. How do you choose? Make a note to yourself on your process.

Expression

Each day for the next week, create an affirmation about what you want to now choose to experience in your life and write it on a piece of paper in script 25 times. (Yes, 25 times!) Make a note of your first affirmation.

Exercises for The Triangle

Illumination

Over the next week, consciously notice the people coming back into or newly entering your life. They each have a message. What is it that they want to share with you regarding possible choices you need to make? Note any relevant insights.

Reflection

Remember two or three significant pieces of feedback you were given that generated big emotional reactions, positively or negatively. What additional messages were contained within that feedback that you can understand more fully now? Why do you need to remember that right now as you move forward in making some key choices in this part of your life? Jot down a few notes.

Expression

Find some privacy. Ask your future self (you 10 years from now) to give you a pep talk out loud. Don't hold back. Say all the great and encouraging things you need to hear right now. Take it in. Feel the energy. What choices and action regarding this area of your life do you want and need to take now? Make a note of it.

Exercises for The Circle

Illumination

Ask two or three members of your advisory board for advice on where you can push yourself further to design a bigger vision for your life experience. What would they encourage you to take on next that you were not willing to consider as one of your choices? Write their advice to you, using their voices.

Reflection

Look back to when you had a big challenge or goal and no idea about how it was going be accomplished. You were overwhelmed. Now that you've achieved it, it may not seem as daunting. What do you know now that you did not know then? How did you work through the challenges and make the tough choices? Write a few words of wisdom.

Expression

Create a short list with three amazing things you want to do, see, or experience in your life before you die. Now, narrow your expected time line to the next three years. Get out a piece of paper, and for each one, write out 10 times "I am so grateful now that I have seen, done, or experienced 'this.'" Repeat this practice each day for the next week. Yes, each day. You may doubt this, but the power that can be unleashed here should not be underestimated. *Thinking it does not count.*

discover box

A Plan of Action for the Discover Box

Having completed at least the exercises in your personalized shape score and perhaps more, you have had a chance to expand your thinking about this area of your life. You have continued to reconnect and build a stronger relationship with yourself after having been stimulated and invited to see your challenges and opportunities through different lenses.

Now is the time when we put your learning into action so you can move yourself forward toward your happiness targets. *So, bring back the coach from within!*

Take a few minutes to review your answers to the aaah-mazing questions and your responses to the experiential exercises. Get yourself grounded, with your mind, heart, and voice all being present together here and now. You are getting yourself in alignment.

You will now be given a chance to map out an action plan for you to shape this part of your life in a way that best serves your desires. Once again, here is how it works:

Happiness Blockers (HB)

Identify the three major obstacles (physical or emotional) you have in this particular area of your life. Write them in the spaces on the action plan page.

Happiness Insights (HI)

On the basis of your answers from the aaah-mazing questions and the experiential exercises, identify three happiness insights that demonstrate your learning and optimism about what is possible for you now to choose and create in your environment. Write them in the spaces on the action plan page.

Happiness Target (HT)

Here is where it all comes together in terms of committing to the changes you will now make to realize your personal growth and experience the happiness you want in this part of your life.

Using your happiness blockers and happiness insights as guides, you are going to define three actions you can take that will be a commitment to you experiencing your happiness in this part of your life. Your happiness targets should be specific and controllable actions you can accomplish. Make sure each of the three happiness targets (goals) is an expansive and empowering commitment for you. They all should be exciting enough to strive for!

Coaching yourself here is about encouraging alignment and choice. Your targets do not have to be perfect selections; just make selections and get out there and experience them!

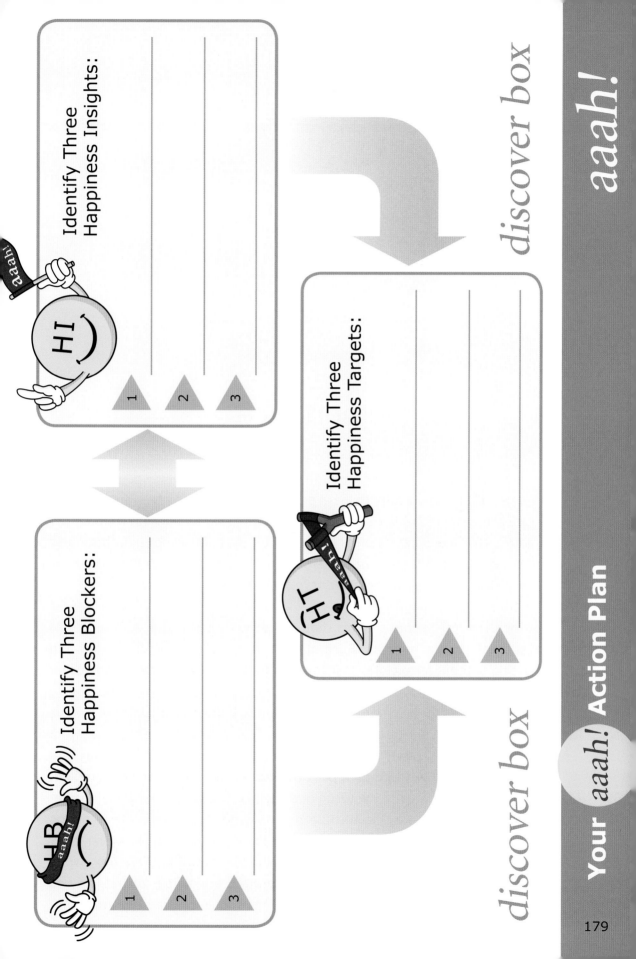

Identify Three
Happiness Insights:

1
2
3

Identify Three
Happiness Blockers:

1
2
3

Identify Three
Happiness Targets:

1
2
3

discover box

discover box

Your *aaah!* **Action Plan**

179

The Unite Box

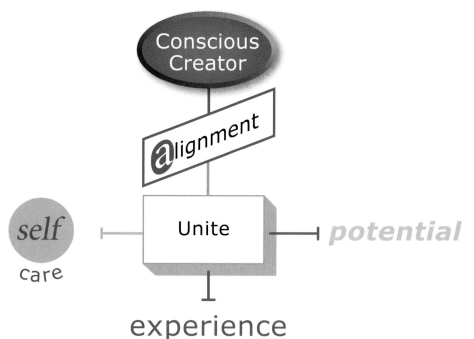

As we travel through the aaah! model, we collect gifts. Each of the stages is a metaphor for moving through our lives conceptually, and each of the boxes is an opportunity to learn something about ourselves and the lives we are choosing to live. The Unite box, however, is different from all the others for me in terms of its beauty. That may sound strange, but *there is something beautiful about embracing yourself as whole and finally allowing all of you to be present in your world without judgment.*

The Unite box acknowledges that we each have a unique set of shadow and light characteristics. Each of them takes a turn in coming out and being present for as long as it takes to fully experience them and accept them as part of you. As you resist, they may persist—as the saying goes. As you ignore them, they continue to come calling and not always at convenient times and places. But if you take the time and work through them, really look at them, and get their message, they are your friends. **They are all a part of you.** Each represents an ingredient that provides flavor to your unique recipe. The key is recognizing that separately they may be terrible or annoying, too much of this or too little of that. Put into the whole mix in the right quantity, however, they add just the right touch to make you who you are. *The Unite box, when unwrapped, contains the perfect, integrated, and whole you*. It is a box to understand and celebrate the true emergence of the **now you**.

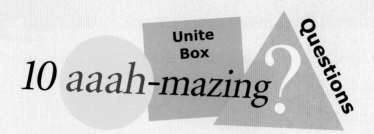

10 aaah-mazing Questions

Unite Box

Remember to stay focused on the area of your life
for which you completed your diagnostic.

1. What will be unleashed when you unite the old you and the new you into the now you? What, if anything, do you fear?

2. What does it feel like to embrace and love the old you for the gifts and experiences it brought so that you could be here now?

3. What does achieving your potential in this area of your life feel and look like?

4. What holds you back from being your authentic true self?

5. What do you want to express but tend to hold back on in this area of your life? How can the now you overcome whatever this is?

6. What do you see as your greatest limitation here? How could it be objectively looked at as a strength?

7. Now that you are expressing yourself from an authentic and integrated perspective, what is available to you to give joyfully to others?

8. What can you claim and experience now that the old you could not?

9. What is your greatest strength from the old you? In your now self, how might that strength be expressed differently? What is available to you in the now expression of this strength?

10. How does it feel to be comfortable in your own skin?

unite box

Exercises for The Square

Illumination

Write the 10 things you know have always been true about you. Now write 10 things you have been trying to change about yourself in this area of your life. On a separate piece of paper, titled your NOW list, make a combined list of five to seven items on which you will focus. At least three must come from each list. Keep a copy of this handy for your reference.

Reflection

You are being roasted for your eightieth birthday. The past 20–25 years have been more exciting than you ever imagined. You have had a successful second career after a satisfying first one. Three people who have known you since your 20s and 30s are speaking at the event. Each one starts his or her roast with one of the following statements. Complete the sentences:

- I never thought …
- If you would have told me …
- Looking back, I can't believe I am standing here now …

Expression

Imagine you are at the end of your life. You are surrounded by those who love you. You want to authentically leave them with a message that you have lived a wonderfully happy life and love them for sharing in the experience with you. What do you need to create for yourself and experience now to ensure that, when that time comes, this can be truth for you without compromise or rationalization? Write your thoughts.

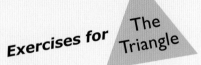

Exercises for The Triangle

Illumination

Imagine that both your old self and your new self are getting into a wet suit together. You both manage to eventually get in there and zip it up, and you start to feel warm and cozy together. You have created a now skin that you are becoming familiar with. What does it feel like? Write five to seven adjectives that describe what this now you would feel like for you to embody and experience in a physical sense.

Reflection

Get in a comfortable quiet place and close your eyes. (Not yet—read the instructions first, of course.) Visualize your ideal now self. Take a close look at you in the now state. What is different? What is the same? Ask your now self what is available to you here that was not available to you in your old self. Ask your now self what you need to do in order to facilitate the process in getting you fully to your now state at this time. Consider the insight received in this experience. What can you do with this moving forward? Make a few notes.

Expression

Write a poem about making peace with yourself. Express how it feels to finally be here, to be able to accept and embrace who you are, and to be proud about the now you who has emerged. Remember to just relax and let it flow from you effortlessly without internal criticism or editing. You may want to start each sentence with the words "I am now....".

Exercises for The Circle

Illumination

Your advisory board has assembled to celebrate the now you. Each group gives you a token gift to remind you of how amazing this accomplishment is because it required you to realize the true potential of who you are. They present you with a box containing four items. Open it. What did each group (the Mentors, the Supporters, the Buddies, the Heroes) put in the box? Make a note of each item.

Reflection

Name the two or three special ingredients in your personal recipe that made the difference in creating the now you. How has your perspective evolved on these ingredients in terms of how you previously viewed them and how you view them now? Write a few notes on this.

Expression

Call a "meeting" of your advisory board and present the members with a brief summary of the now you. You have only few minutes to highlight what the experience of getting here has been like. To help you keep your comments brief and memorable, you develop an acronym that you tell them will always serve as a reminder to you (e.g., NOW: the (N)OW me is an (O)VERWHELMINGLY (W)ONDERFUL experience). What is your personal acronym, and how can you use it to sustain your feeling? Write few notes.

aaah!

unite box

A Plan of Action for the Unite Box

For more detailed instructions, please refer to the Discover box.

On the basis of your answers to the aaah-mazing questions and your responses to the experiential exercises, you are going to develop an action plan for forward movement.

Happiness Blockers (HB)

Identify the three major obstacles (physical or emotional) you have in this particular area of your life. Write them in the spaces on the action plan page.

Happiness Insights (HI)

On the basis of your answers from the aaah-mazing questions and the experiential exercises, identify three happiness insights that demonstrate your optimism about what is possible for you in terms of reaching your personal potential in your environment. Write them in the spaces on the action plan page.

Happiness Target (HT)

Now define three actions you can take that will be a commitment to you moving toward what your potential is for the now you in this area of your life. Make them things you can, in fact, control and accomplish. Make them exciting enough to strive for!

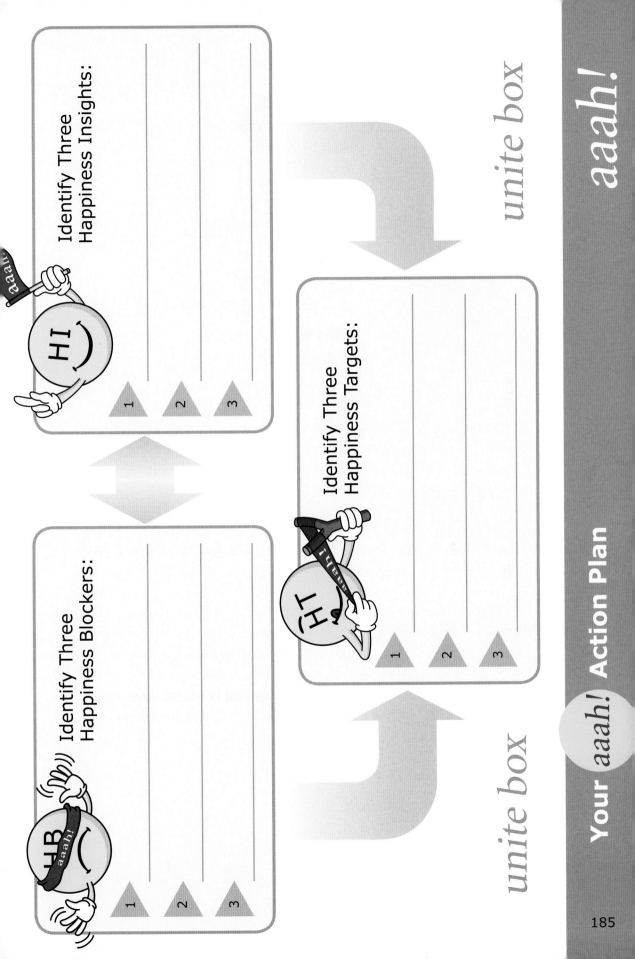

Identify Three
Happiness Insights:

1
2
3

Identify Three
Happiness Blockers:

1
2
3

Identify Three
Happiness Targets:

1
2
3

unite box

unite box

Your *aaah!* Action Plan

aaah!

185

The Destiny Box

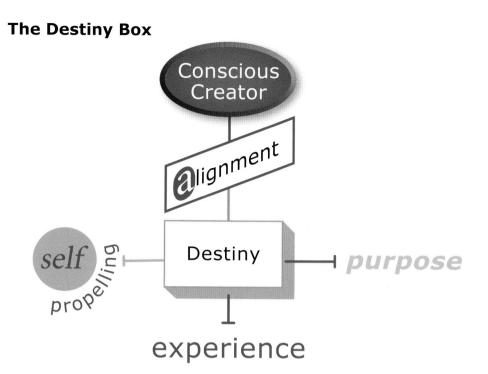

Despite some preconceived notions or judgments, the Destiny box is just another box in the aaah! model. For some of you, when you saw the model for the first time, you might have thought, "How do I get there? And, if I can just get there, the other pieces will fall into place, right?"

I hope you know now from your experience with the aaah! model that even if your Destiny box had a circle in it, you may not have been able to fully experience it because other boxes may have had you stuck.

The Destiny box is, however, special in its own way. It has the energy of feeling open, flowing, and comfortable for us. *It is our unique place.* Unlike a destination that gives you the sense of stopping, we are not sitting in the Destiny box and resting on our laurels; we are constantly moving and seeing how we can further expand the energy we seem to be creating for ourselves and feel so right in. How do we keep the flow going and continue our purposeful work here? *We keep riding the roller coaster.*

We know that part of the process of living our destiny is continually taking a ride on our roller coaster of life and moving into our next **circulinear** process through the model as we continue to change and grow. The Destiny box acknowledges a complete loop for us. It may have been made up of many smaller loops, but it is a pause box, not a hard stop. *We never stop creating; we just keep expanding the circle of where we are.*

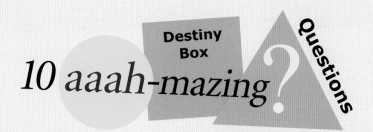

Remember to stay focused on the area of your life
for which you completed your diagnostic.

1. Consider where you are now in this area of your life.
   Look around. Make a mental note. What is a natural expansion
   from here?

2. Which one word captures your purpose in this area of your life?

3. What message has been trying to get through in this part of your
   life that you can only now hear?

4. What does being in continuous flow mean to you here?

5. What have you learned about happiness here?

6. How can you stay conscious of the continuing messages that
   come into your life to further guide you and help you evolve in
   your purpose?

7. When you are quietly thanking your God/the universe for your
   gifts and experiences in this life, what do you know now to be
   most important to you?

8. What do you need to know to allow yourself to fully experience
   trust, freedom, and abundance in your life?

9. What does it feel like to live your life on purpose and with
   purpose every day?

10. What do you now say out loud to yourself or others that is a
    new expression of who you have become?

Tools and Treasures

Exercises for The Square

Illumination

An auditorium full of people has been waiting anxiously to experience you. The announcer states, "Ladies and gentlemen, now the moment you have all been waiting for …." What is it that you are meant to do/say/demonstrate to this audience? Allow the answer to come to you intuitively and naturally, and do not overthink this. Write a few words on what you are called to do.

Reflection

Stay with the example above. What is the first impression you want to make? Take note of this.

Expression

Stay with the example above. After you complete your activity, you are asked a question. The request is for you to give your perspective on what it takes to create a life full of experiences that are purposeful and joyful. You smile and offer the following words of wisdom. Write them here.

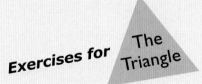

Exercises for The Triangle

Illumination

Find your favorite picture of you as a child. Look at it closely. Notice your eyes, your expression. What was known to that child then that you can now see that has insight for what you were meant to experience in your life? How can you live the essence of what that child knew in an integrated and authentic way now? Make a few notes.

Reflection

You have intuitively received messages throughout your life, which have been confirmed by others, regarding what you should be experiencing in this area of your life. You know they're true, but you have shrugged them off as not being practical. What is the essence of what has always been there that you can bring into your life now? Make a few notes.

Expression

Change the question in your mind that challenges whether what calls to you in this part of your life is right to a declarative statement that expresses your commitment to make it your experience. Write your declarative statement.

Exercises for The Circle

Illumination

What wisdom can you give others about what it looks and feels like to experience your destiny based on the journey you have traveled? What should they watch for as confirmation that they are in the right place? Make a few notes.

Reflection

Looking back, what messages did people bring to you that foreshadowed things to come in your life regarding your destiny in this area? Did you believe then that these messages were true for you and in alignment with your dreams? Make a few notes.

Expression

As you enjoy the experience of living your life on purpose and with purpose, what can you share with others in terms of what you have learned about trust, freedom of expression, and abundance based on your life lessons on your path to fulfillment? Make a few notes.

destiny box

A Plan of Action for the Destiny Box

For more detailed instructions, refer to the Discover box.

On the basis of your answers to the aaah-mazing questions and your responses to the experiential exercises, you are going to develop an action plan for forward movement.

Happiness Blockers (HB)

Identify the three obstacles (physical or emotional) you have in this particular area of your life. Write them in the spaces on the action plan page.

Happiness Insights (HI)

On the basis of your answers from the questions and the experiential exercises, identify three happiness insights that demonstrate your energetic pull toward your purpose and what you want to be experiencing in this part of your life. Write them in the spaces on the action plan page.

Happiness Targets (HT)

Now define three actions you can take that will be a commitment to experience what your purpose and destiny are in this area of your life. Make them things you can, in fact, control and accomplish. Make them exciting enough to strive for!

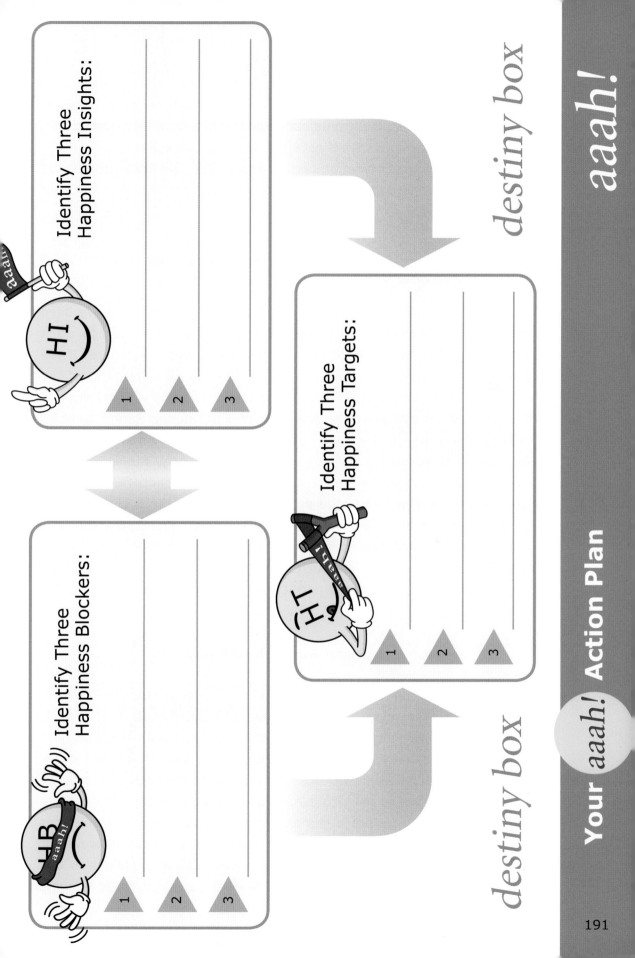

Identify Three
Happiness Insights:

1
2
3

destiny box

Identify Three
Happiness Blockers:

1
2
3

Identify Three
Happiness Targets:

1
2
3

destiny box

Your *aaah!* Action Plan

191

The Major *Alignment* Takeaways

In the Conscious Creator stage, you are being called into *partnership with yourself*. Having spent time building up this critical relationship with yourself, now is when you are asked to put it into practice. You will also need to coach yourself through certain areas. *The goal is to integrate all that you have learned and discovered about you and to now step into your life and experience it the way you want.*

aaah! **Discover and choose which experience you want to have now**

You have been traveling a path throughout your life. It may have been unconsciously chosen to this point, but now you are ready to do it consciously. So what will you choose? What is available to you here? If you are like most people, the answers are "I don't know" and "too much." The many choices and possibilities create indecision. Maybe I will try a little of this or a little of that and then decide which I like better. Sound familiar? Well, the hard truth is that this is a prescription for frustration and lack of movement. The environment around you is full of possibilities—yes, that is true. But you now know more about who you are and what you want. **It is time to take action, and that action is to choose**. **It is that simple.** Look around, see what is there, and choose something. Take a shot and go for a full, not partial, experience. If it is not an experience you enjoy, choose again. The phrase "Get a life" is great. Just replace "a life" with "an experience" and you have the perfect inspiration for yourself here: "**Get an experience**."

aaah! **Be your integrated and authentic now self**

We are always going to be a mix of our old and new selves. The ability to integrate, embrace, and enter into our now self is the ultimate in alignment. Sure, major pieces get adjusted over time, but we can always look back on our childhood and see an essence of something there that never leaves us. It might not be what we like. It could be that know-it-all look we have or that annoying roll of our eyes back into our heads when we are bored with others. We are a composite of old and new that transforms and evolves over time. *What being our now self is all about, however, is being aware of and accepting of who we are and loving ourselves as well as understanding the power we create when we allow all of us to come forward in the world.*

We are all unique with our strengths and weaknesses. We have both shadow and light in our personalities. What we often fail to recognize, however, is that the combination of these creates our authentic selves. Only we have the perspective or capability to see and create something that may not have been there before, either for us alone or for the world at large. If we don't embrace our old and new selves in creating who we are now, we leave out part of the potential magic that we have within us and can bring forward to voice in the world as we create our experiences.

aaah! *Live your life on purpose*

The Conscious Creator has a strong sense of living in a world that is relative, not absolute. Being in alignment so that things flow and allowing direction to take shape are processes whereby we hold onto the handlebars for support—but not too tightly. Living our lives on purpose is similar. We would all like to believe that there is an absolute *something* set in stone that we are supposed to do in this life. *The hard truth is that it is not that specific or even important, for that matter.* We are here to live our lives and to experience them, and we create those experiences we want based on being consciously aware of, sensing, responding to, and claiming those things that we want to experience. We have an inner knowing of where we need to be heading. The essence of our dream is with us, and we discover through our experiences whether we are on or off target. Our job is to notice, feel, and redirect so that we can align ourselves with the flow of our own energy and ensure that we stay on the right path for us.

Living our destinies is a little like growing up. When we are kids, we have behaviors and actions that may or may not work for us, but we experiment, we experience, and we adjust. The process of adjusting and selecting better experiences that produce the results we were looking for is called growing up and maturing. As adults, and as Curious Seekers, Courageous Finders, and, ultimately, Conscious Creators moving through *selfhood*, we learn that we must keep growing. There is no stopping. To live our destiny is to live the life we want to experience each and every day until we embody the learning we came here to experience. **This is unique for all of us, and it is a process we call our journey.** As we travel, we need to continue to shape the change we encounter into the growth we want on purpose!

CHAPTER *11*

Integrating the Practice of aaah! *into Daily Life*

The purpose of any practice is to become so familiar and comfortable with it that you integrate it into your subconscious, thus making your behavior automatic and natural. We can have these experiences with driving, riding a bicycle, playing a musical instrument, or even coaching ourselves.

Developing your personalized practice of aaah! requires that you choose to use your skills of awareness, acceptance, and alignment until they are integrated into your being and become as natural to you as breathing deeply.

aaah! **Is a Life Tool**

Our lives are dynamic, constantly flowing and changing, so predicting what we will be confronted with in our day-to-day activities is impossible. Having immediate access to *a **life tool*** such as aaah! connects us to a simple and powerful process we can use in the moment as we work through our responses to situations and circumstances. It can assist us in calibrating where we are relative to where we want to be.

The aaah! diagnostic will be a valuable reference for you to track and monitor your personal transformation over time. By going back periodically to review your old and new personalized charts for the different areas of your life, you will be able to see whether and where movement from squares to triangles, and ultimately to circles, has occurred. This will allow you to continuously monitor how well you are shaping your growth and change. You can also then go back and redo some of the exercises to experience new insights and learning that can further accelerate your progress.

Through this journey, you have also developed and practiced important life skills that will further serve to support you in your growth and change process. These skills are always available to you, and in selecting to use them, you are choosing your responses to events and are creating the experiences you want to have. ***The aaah! life tool provides you with an easy-to-remember and actionable checklist in your pursuit of happiness:***

*a*wareness: What do you need to be mindful of in this situation that can provide you with insights into your needs, desires, and choices?

*a*cceptance: What do you need to accept here by letting go, forgiving, or embracing—which can otherwise block your happiness?

*a*lignment: What do you need to align with here (thoughts, feelings, expressions) to create and allow your happiness experience to occur?

*h*appiness!: Are you clear on what you want, and are you ready to choose?

Having traveled this far, you are now ready to get out there and create your experiences, right? I am choosing to sense an enthusiastic *Yes*! To further help you integrate the practice of aaah! into your real life in real time, however, we are going to end our journey together with some practical reminders and suggestions you can easily use.

Rituals, Routines, and Structures

In my coaching practice, I encourage my clients to **use *environmental reminders* to facilitate the integration of change** into their lives. These are called structures when they are physical and visible, but they can just as easily be routines or rituals that are practiced. The goal is to ensure that a desired thought process or behavior is regularly reinforced through having physical and emotional reminders surrounding us. One popular weight loss program, for example, awards a small key ring after losing a certain amount of weight. Customers are encouraged to use the key ring as a visible reminder of their accomplishments when they might be tempted to overindulge or skip exercising. When we are tired or hungry, forgetting how critical it is to maintain good habits is easy. The key ring is a reminder, a structure integrated into daily life that is capable of stimulating a physical and emotional connection to a goal.

Another approach is integrating a ritual into your day. You may find that when you first wake up, even before getting out of bed, is a great time for you to get centered and focused on your intentions for the day. What will you choose to feel and experience today? What if you set an intention to enjoy all of the activities in your day, even though you know your schedule is overbooked? You may choose to be mindful of the gifts and messages that come to you through interactions with different people on this day. *By taking a few moments to consciously set your intentions, you are telling yourself what you want to experience.*

You will be surprised at the power of this act. The combination of consciously being aware of your intentions, emotionally connecting to what you want to experience, and expressing this to yourself uses the practice of aaah! before you get out of bed in the morning. This ritual alone provides you with a higher likelihood of experiencing the happiness you have targeted for this day.

Of course, morning might not be the best time for you. Instead, you may need to close your office door for a few minutes each day and focus on your intentions. Or you may need to use the train ride home or the drive time while you pick the kids up from soccer practice. The where and when don't matter as much as does putting a few minutes aside to do it daily. That is what makes it a ritual. *This is personal, intimate time for you, so enjoy it.*

How about silently acknowledging what you are grateful for in your life? It's easy to do and keeps positive energy circulating around and through you. As your brush your teeth, take the dog for a walk, or enjoy that first sip of coffee, the expression of gratitude puts you right into an experience of happiness and can further remind you of your happiness targets in other areas of your life.

Routines can also help to integrate the practice of aaah! into your life. The difference between a ritual and a routine is that a routine has a set sequence of actions. Taking a shower, making coffee, getting dressed, and even driving ourselves to work are all routines. We tend to complete the same steps in the same order whenever we do them. They become practiced behaviors that are integrated into our lives. Within this sequence, we can easily choose an entry point and say, "Okay, when I get into the shower each morning, I will set my intentions for the day or choose my happiness target." Because you are inserting your practice of aaah! within an already established sequence of events, you have a higher likelihood for ensuring it is done daily. You may also insert a short mental review on what you learned yesterday that can help you today. For example, did you notice any happiness insights or happiness blockers? Just choose an entry point and within a short time, you will have inserted your practice of aaah! into your routine.

You know that special photograph that brings a smile to your face, maybe a family reunion photograph that makes you laugh? This is a structure that reconnects you to a happiness target. Another structure could be printing out your **personal declaration statement** you completed in the Courageous Finder chapter and hanging it on your bathroom mirror or in your office where you will see it regularly. This provides you with a consistent reminder of your intentions across your physical, intellectual, emotional, and spiritual goals. I do this!

One structure I created for myself during a stressful time was bringing Tazo Calm tea bags into my marathon day-long management team meetings. I would have several bags as a constant reminder to stay calm, be patient, and control myself emotionally. This was extremely helpful and became something other people on my team noticed. Sometimes others asked where my tea bags were; apparently, they had become structures for them, too!

You might also choose to simply put a Post-it note on your computer that says "aaah!" to remind you to look for opportunities to acknowledge, create, and experience your daily practice. Creating structures can be fun. Play with the idea and see what works for you.

It's Okay—Even Mandatory—to Be _self_-centered!

In our culture, being openly self-centered is frowned upon. In the practice of aaah!, however, we are in a state of **selfhood.** We are determined to create and experience our lives on purpose, which is a radical act most people will not choose. **Being self-centered, or centered in ourselves, is a state of grounded, purposeful strength.** When we are centered within ourselves and experiencing the happiness of our lives, we are able to interact with others in positive, meaningful, and authentic ways. Life is all about relationships. The sequence is getting our relationship right with ourselves so we can bring our best selves forward in our interactions with others.

self discovery **and the search for what is** aaah!**-vailable**

We need to constantly scan our environments for what is possible now. Our focus on self-discovery should be activated as we notice changes in the environment and identify new possibilities emerging as opportunities for personal growth and new happiness targets.

self care **and the realization of our personalized** aaah!**-pportunities**

Our beliefs create our boundaries for realizing our personal potential. _Selecting big, empowering beliefs for our lives is taking care of ourselves._ We are creating the space for the expansion and growth of who we are into who we can potentially be. We must accept our ability to achieve anything and everything we set our hearts and minds to, and we must not allow playing small or self-limiting beliefs to get in our way. Our ability to realize our personal growth potential is unlimited.

self propelling **toward our** aaah!**-ccomplishments**

The dreams we promise ourselves create an unyielding self-propelling energy that carries us forward in our lives. Once set in motion by the clarity of what we want, we are compelled to create our path and move toward our purpose. _Fulfilling our dreams is our destiny_. The practice of

aaah!

199

aaah! is the process of continuously moving into the experiences of our missions, purposes, and goals moment by moment through the course of our lives. Remember to keep going and to keep growing!

Coaching the Ongoing Relationship with Yourself

To be in a state of aaah! while engaging in your busy life, you are going to have to rely heavily on your self-coaching techniques and the strength of the relationship you have built with yourself.

Remember to meet yourself where you are and get grounded before you go anywhere. Sometimes just experiencing the excitement or negativity of a situation is what is called for as we allow ourselves to embrace a full spectrum of emotional experiences in life. Once we process and allow some time with the feeling, we can choose to move ourselves forward. As emotions get activated within us, we should also coach ourselves through the appropriate expression and release so as not to create resistance and negative health consequences. Whether that be verbal or creative expression, journaling, or exercising, our coach within should be encouraging us to **process and release**. *Calling upon our skills of awareness, acceptance, and alignment is the role of our inner coach.*

You will need to keep the ego, saboteurs, and gremlins at bay to amplify the voice of your true self or inner wisdom on a regular basis. Once these voices are at the right levels, **don't hesitate to call yourself forth to live big!** We are here to go after our life experiences, not to play small on the sidelines.

Coaching yourself in the moment is a challenging task. You may be emotionally charged with momentum in a negative direction, and you may be on a slippery slope with limited traction. Here, however, your skills of awareness and the strength of your relationship with yourself will serve you well. Tap into them, call yourself on your own behavior, and just pause for a moment and get perspective. Remember that you can choose to respond in whatever way you want in any circumstances you may find yourself. You can choose whether you want to experience frustration and anger in this moment or whether you can accept it and let it go. At every opportunity, stay present in coaching yourself into a state of aaah!

> ### *aaah* Breathing Exercise
>
> Use your breathing as a structure. Notice how shallow or fast your breaths may be. Take some longer, deeper breaths and slow down the adrenaline production that may be causing you stress. Allow yourself to experience your breathing with focus and intent. Become aware of the changes in your emotional and physical being. Take time often with this exercise.

Scope out the Situation and Take in a New Perspective

Occasionally, you are going to be in situations where both proactive and reactive responses are necessary to get you into a state of aaah! We can't choose the events that surround us, but we can choose our responses to them. Sometimes we are so engaged both mentally and emotionally in a situation that we lose our perspective and therefore cannot decide what choice to make in our own best interest. So how do we approach this type of situation? I use *a technique I call scoping.*

Any perspective we have on a situation is just one of many. What gets us stuck typically is seeing one perspective clearly and shutting down all other considerations. To coach ourselves through this, I like to use three scopes: a microscope, a periscope, and a telescope.

The microscope perspective is one in which we need to clarify our focus. Either we can be too close to a situation and need to pull back or we are too far away and need to come in closer to get more details. We use our microscope perspective when everything seems to be a blur and we are not sure what we see. Our skill of awareness helps here because with focus and some slight adjustments, we can quickly gain an observer perspective, without the confusion, of what we are really looking at.

The periscope view of the situation is one in which we can surround an issue and see it from several vantage points, like a submarine at the surface of the water before emerging. We get a peripheral view of the area immediately around us from all sides, so we are not locked in. We can safely examine the range of the possible choices prior to committing and can get a sense of how close or far away these various options may be.

The telescope view is one that allows us to take a step back and create some distance between ourselves and the emotions surrounding an issue. We can then focus and zoom in safely to take a closer look. This spatial orientation allows the opportunity of introspection without external influences surrounding us and creating noise and distractions.

Once we have proactively and reactively examined the situation from different perspectives, we can move ourselves into a position of choice. This will allow us to experience our happiness target and therefore bring us into a state of aaah!

Our Relationships Create Our Experiences

Our relationships with others, whether positive or negative, originate from our relationships with ourselves. **People are our mirrors**. We may or may not like what we see; our challenge is to become aware of what we are seeing and the effect it may be having on our lives.

The practice of aaah! has empowered us to be more conscious of our choices, especially as we are thrust into our daily encounters with the fast-paced dynamics of life, people and their stories. Your challenge remains the same: experience your life by choosing happiness for yourself in each moment. As others come into your world and create events and energy to surround you, remember your skills of aaah! Eventually, you will be comfortable enough to share them with others. After all, you are an experienced coach now.

aaah!-pportunities for You!

Now that you have the basics down, how will you choose to integrate the practice of aaah! in your own life? Remember to:

Stay *aaah!*-lert

Use your skills of awareness every day. Observe your environment. Do you see changes that can provide you with opportunities for growth? Are you connected to yourself and your feelings, or are you slipping away into your head? Are you reaching for a tangible thing to hold, or are you focused on an experience you want to have? Notice what you are doing and feeling, and make your choices in a mindful and purposeful way. Also, if you are not happy from time to time on your journey, that is not the worst thing that can happen to you. No, the worst thing is the physical and psychological burden that results from being trapped in unhappiness and the health effects it can have if you don't use your skills of awareness, acceptance, and alignment to steer a course toward happiness. So remember that getting stuck is expected—staying stuck is not!

Choose to be *aaah!*-wake

Even though it can be challenging, embrace your new state of *selfhood* and consciousness. You may feel the temptation to retreat into a lower state of consciousness, close your eyes and take a short nap, or slip back into focusing on others and not yourself. Stay awake and engaged in your practice of aaah! Use your structures, routines, and rituals to remind you to get present if you have drifted off and lost some ground. *The most important thing we can do is wake up and get back into practice as quickly as possible. No lectures, no beating ourselves up—just get back on track.* Each day and each moment are new opportunities to choose happiness.

Rely on your *aaah!*-bilities

You can choose happiness, regardless of your current circumstances, and you can now use the aaah! practice to help guide you and keep you there. Things are going to feel overwhelming at times. Life may be too much, coming at you too fast, and you might not be able to get traction. So what do you do? First, just acknowledge that whatever this experience is, it is temporary. *That is why our work is ongoing and continuous.* Whether opportunity or challenge is in front of us, it is only a temporary time upon which we can create an experience. Remember also that no matter how good or bad things are, your **aaah-bility** to experience the entire spectrum of emotion is what life is about. So, if a bad time is here now, as hard as it is, take a deep breath and use your skills to see what is here in this moment for you that offers insight and learning in your life. *Hidden within this is something to learn. Be curious and courageous enough to find out what is there.* Get yourself aligned with the energy so you can choose to fully experience what is here now and process it. Then, choose to either stay here or move on to another experience if that is what you desire. *Our lives are processes. The practice of aaah! helps you to streamline the process of choosing happiness purposefully and consistently!*

Believe in the concept of aaah!-bundance

 Everything you need is within you, always! All that you need to create what you want is here. Don't hesitate to dream big. This is your life, your experience. Use your practice of aaah! to keep you on track. Take every change as a chance to shape your life purpose and always be happy!

Life is just aaah-mazing!

aaah!

Epilogue

You are now ready to begin your personalized *practice of aaah!* as an experienced *life shaper*. In addition to the answers that you've always had inside of you, you have the aaah! diagnostic tool and model to help guide you through the continuous process of change and growth. But don't expect it all to fall into place right out of the gate. After all, this is a practice, not perfection, so be prepared for some *circulinear* loops.

Like the muscles you need to build in order to acquire strength, your practice of aaah! will build up your comfort and confidence with the principles you've learned here. You'll begin to recognize when you're sabotaging yourself and making choices that aren't in alignment with your true desires. Eventually, your aaah! practice will become automatic, and using your skills of awareness, acceptance, and alignment will be like breathing: continuous and natural. Being able to call yourself forth into *a state of aaah!* on a moment's notice gives you the confidence to allow yourself to boldly live your life without limits as the Curious Seeker, the Courageous Finder, and the Conscious Creator.

For now, begin using the diagnostic and model to take snapshots of specific, focused segments of your life. You may find that as you use the diagnostic in different areas, you will see some patterns emerge. This kind of big-picture understanding comes with regular use. Over time, you'll see shifts in your priorities and responses. Keep using the model to drive you forward and remember to spend time reflecting and processing your learning to reveal the true essence of what you want in your life.

As you make progress in your journey, you may want to enlist others to help you. Many people who begin the self-coaching process find value in working with a professional coach or therapist to help accelerate, dive deeper, or navigate through particularly troublesome areas. As a leadership coach, I can tell you that this kind of assistance can be invaluable, even for short periods of time. Sometimes, what you need is an objective third party to help push you, pull you, or just be with you through the process!

Of course, a book is one way to experience the practice of aaah!—and I hope that the visual and interactive nature was responsive to your individual learning needs. But because I believe in providing opportunities to *surround you* with the experience of aaah!, I want to invite you to visit the ***interactive aaah! practice center*** at:

http://www.openupandsayaaah.com

Here, you'll find material to supplement the book and to help you continue on your journey of aaah! You can learn about my coaching and speaking engagements, as well as new information about leading yourself through the change and personal growth process as you pursue happiness and well-being. I hope you'll visit. And, please, share your stories. I believe that we can all learn from each other, and I would love to hear about how *Open up and Say aaah!* has helped you in your journey toward happiness. You can find my web site and contact me at:

http://www.ericapeitler.com

I hope that this book has been meaningful to you and that you feel the benefits of *the practice of aaah!* already. It is my great privilege to help readers shape the changes in their lives into the growth and happiness they want to experience and, in doing so, to help them reach their personal potential. I believe that one important component of this is a consistent and regular practice of aaah!

For now, take good care of yourself.

All my best,

Erica Peitler

About the Author

Erica Peitler is a pharmacist and an internationally respected business leader with 20 years of experience as a corporate transformational change agent. With an executive VP/general management background spanning operational division management assignments, board-level strategic initiatives, and chief scientific officer roles, Erica has been selected throughout her professional career to lead, grow, and transform brands, people, and organizations.

Now, as a professionally trained and certified leadership coach, Erica is pursuing her passion for helping people orchestrate personal transformational changes as they discover who they are—and who they are becoming—as leaders. With an engaging, provocative, and fun style, Erica helps leaders shape their growth potential by reaching beyond their comfort levels and imaginations as they pursue becoming all that they desire to be in their personal and professional lives.

As a keynote speaker and author, Erica educates, entertains, and enlightens audiences on leadership, transformational change, and personal/professional growth initiatives.

Erica is also a group chair with Vistage International, the largest CEO membership organization in the world, with more than 15,000 members in 16 countries.

She resides in Morristown, New Jersey.

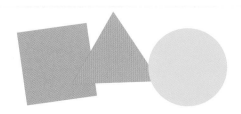

Index

Index

Index

Index

Index

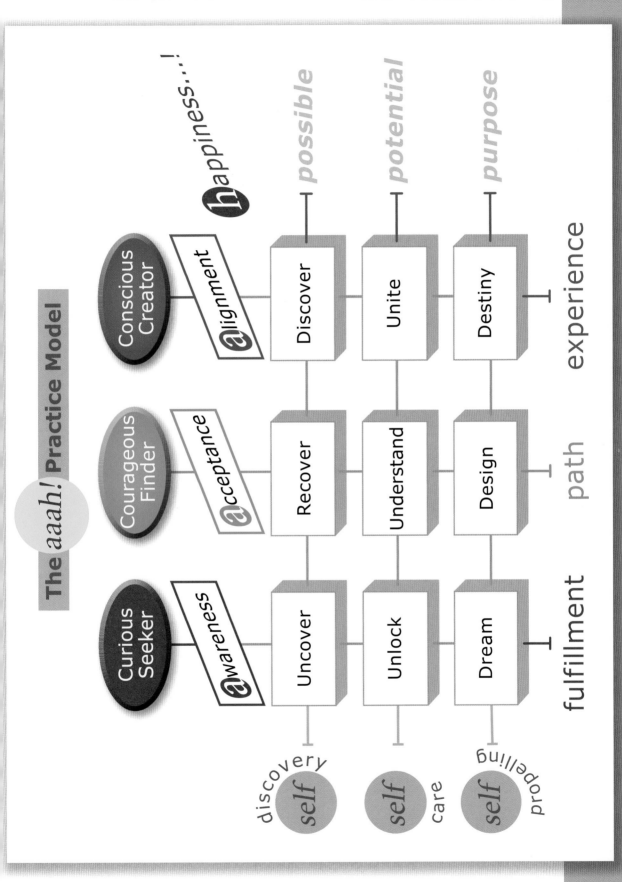

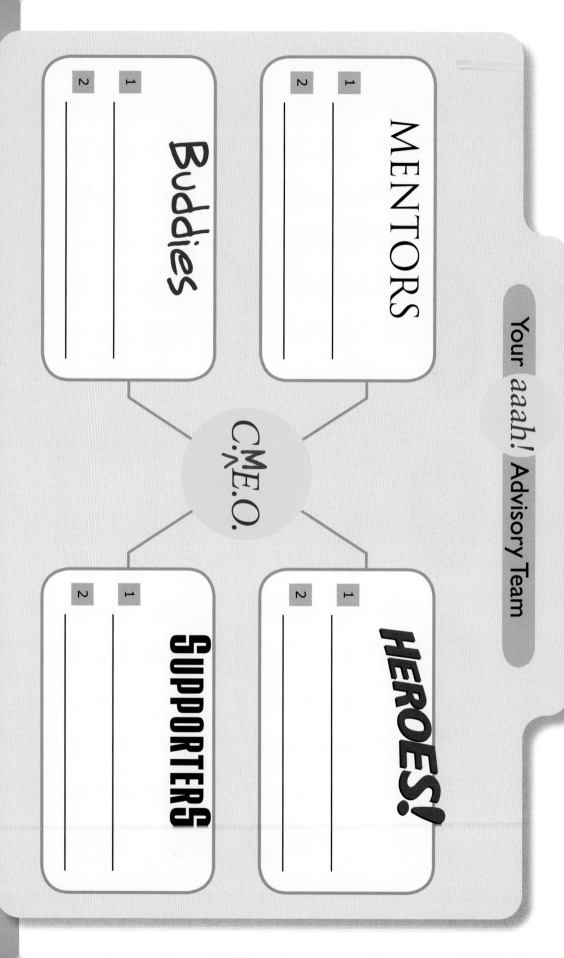

Your aaah! Advisory Team

MENTORS

1
2

Buddies

1
2

C.M.E.O.

HEROES!

1
2

SUPPORTERS

1
2